The Elusive
Father Brown

The Life of Mgr John O'Connor

To the memory of Monsignor John Joseph O'Connor who sometimes looked over my shoulder and nudged me in the right direction.

The Elusive
Father Brown

The Life of Mgr John O'Connor

Julia Smith

Julia Smith

GRACEWING

First published in 2010

Gracewing
2 Southern Avenue
Leominster
Herefordshire HR6 0QF

ISBN 978 0 85244 698 0

Typeset by Action Publishing Technology Ltd, Gloucester GL1 5SR

Contents

List of Illustrations

Photographs 1, 2, 5,7–9, 11, 13–18, 20, 22–27
by author, 4, 6 by David Smith

Foreword

In St Paul's Cathedral, the memorial to its architect, Sir Christopher Wren, reads, *Si monumentum requiris, circumspice* (If you need a monument, look around you); the whole building speaks of him. It wouldn't be inappropriate to apply those words to Mgr John O'Connor, in respect of the second church which he built, Our Lady & First Martyrs, Bradford, and not only because of its 'round' shape (although it is in fact, octagonal: a fact he wasn't slow to point out!). First Martyrs was not the only – or even the first – church, that Mgr O'Connor had built. That honour goes to the Holy Spirit, Heckmondwike (in the shape of a Greek cross), also in the Diocese of Leeds.

Of course, there was much more to John O'Connor than the building and beautifying of churches, as this excellent book bears witness. He walked the moors with G. K. Chesterton, whom he received into full communion with the Catholic Church (and in time became the inspiration for G. K.'s famous *Father Brown*). He encouraged and commissioned Eric Gill (whose fine Stations of the Cross adorn St Cuthbert's church together with statues in both that building and First Martyrs). He read papers to the Bradford Athenaeum Club and was a member of the Cartwright Hall Art Gallery Committee. Here is a man of broad sympathies and understanding; a twentieth-century Renaissance Man if ever there was one!

Yet, Mgr O'Connor was first and foremost a parish priest, and the following pages give us a glimpse of his devotion to that vocation. His love of the liturgy (not forgetting his *avant garde* views!) and his dedication to the needy of the parish were part of what made him the fine pastor that he was.

Although he died in 1952, *The Elusive Father Brown* is still remembered here with affection. Julia Smith's fine biography serves to remind us of what a great person he was and how his legacy is all around us. The year 2010 sees the seventy-fifth anniversary of the opening of First Martyrs' church. The publication of this book is a wonderful preparation for the celebrations!

Philip Moger, parish priest
St Cuthbert & First Martyrs of Rome
Feast of the Visitation of the BVM, 2008

Preface

I have always known that the real-life counterpart of Father Brown, G. K. Chesterton's fictional detective-priest, was Father O'Connor, St Cuthbert's non-fictional parish priest. I must have absorbed this information, and much more, by a sort of osmosis when, as a child, I waded through every book on my parents' and grandparents' bookshelves. Everything from Arthur Mee's *The Children's Encyclopaedia,* to Zane Grey's stories of the Wild West, presumably meeting Chesterton somewhere along the way.

Living in the same city as Father O'Connor, Bradford in the West Riding (as it then was) of Yorkshire, may have caused that fact to linger in my brain longer than some. Many years later, after becoming a regular contributor to a number of Yorkshire periodicals, I thought it time I found out more about Fathers O'Connor and Brown.

If I had lived in his Heaton parish, I might have met Father O'Connor, as it was he had died some forty years previously but I was able to find enough material to write three thousand or so words about *The Man Who Was Father Brown.* This only served to show me that I really knew tantalizingly little about the man and whetted my appetite for further research into his truly dichotomous life.

I realized I was starting the project not a moment too soon when I began to discover people who had known the priest but were now in their seventies and eighties, parishioners, ex-altar boys, his one-time curate, past pupils of St Joseph's College for Girls and the boys' school, St Bede's, and the nurse who looked after him during his last illness. Sadly, I have taken too long to finish the project as some of the people I interviewed have since died.

Although past pupils recalled Father O'Connor being accompanied at times by G. K. Chesterton, Hilaire Belloc, or other famous friends, and the parishioners were aware of their good fortune in possessing a set of Stations of the Cross carved by Eric Gill, they had no idea of the esteem in which their parish priest was held by his famous contemporaries in the wider world of the arts both at home and abroad.

Father O'Connor is an elusive character, a shadow that flits briefly through the indexes of other peoples' biographies. He corresponded regularly with the Chestertons, especially with Frances, Mrs Chesterton, who confided intimate details of her gynaecological problems in her letters to him, something she would not normally dream of discussing with anyone. Eric Gill was not so shy of discussing anything of a sexual nature, as his Diaries testify, but it was to this particular Catholic priest he preferred to confess his transgressions, and then discuss his problems with him over a drink and a smoke in the presbytery.

Father Ronald Knox was happy when he heard that Chesterton had sent for Father O'Connor to discuss serious concerns that were troubling him. He thought that Father Brown's powers of neglecting his parish seemed even more admirable than Dr Watson's powers of neglecting his practice and hoped the trait was drawn from life. Certainly the priest seemed able to rush here, there and everywhere at a moment's notice, but according to his parishioners, it never impinged on his parish duties.

Maisie Ward, G. K. Chesterton's biographer, suggested that his friendship with the real-life counterpart of his fictional creation was perhaps the closest of Chesterton's life, with a unique atmosphere of confidence and intimacy between them 'that was all the more convincing by the very absence of all parade of it'.[1] This seems to be the key to his personality, appearing in the lives of the great and the good, even the not so good, without any fuss, completely accepted and at home in whatever particular circles he found himself. A forceful character, once met never forgotten, who somehow managed to remain a very quiet man, grounded in his strong, but simple, faith.

So who was this shadowy, enigmatic figure? With the help of his own unpublished childhood memoirs, his correspondence with Charles Gatty, Gilbert and Frances Chesterton, Dame Werburg Welch, and the diaries and letters of Eric Gill, my mission has been to enable Father O'Connor to take his rightful place alongside his intellectual contemporaries. I hope I have been successful.

Notes
1. Ward, *Gilbert Keith Chesterton*.

Acknowledgements

I would like to thank all those who knew Father O'Connor personally and kindly shared their memories with me by letter, telephone, e-mail or by granting me an interview. Especial thanks go to Margaret Rossiter for giving me an excellent guided tour of Clonmel.

For answering my queries, obtaining, photocopying or giving permission to quote from material, my thanks go to Revd John Abberton, Church of the Holy Spirit, Heckmondwike; Bingley Public Library; Joan Bond, Catholic National Library, Farnborough; Bradford Local History Library, British Library, Manuscript and Rare Books Dept, London; Brú Ború Cultural Centre, Cashel; Richard Carter, Gabrielle Earnshaw and Noel McFerran, John Kelly Library, University of St Michael's College, Toronto; Cleckheaton Public Library; Jim Coffey, St Bede's Grammar School, Bradford; Fr Pat Conlan, Dublin; Alan Crookham, National Gallery, London; Revd Michael Dolan and staff, Talbot Library, Preston; Robert Finnigan, Leeds Diocesan Archives; Natalie Franklin, Ditchling Museum; John G. Frith, Bradford Athenaeum Society; General Register Office, Dublin; Sr M. Gregory, Bar Convent, York; Henry Moore Institute, Leeds; Ilkley Public Library; Joanna Jackson, St Joseph's College, Bradford; Dom Philip Jebb and Dom Daniel Rees, Downside Abbey; Sr Mary Joseph and Nick Schofield, Venerable English College, Rome; Keighley Local History Library; Gilbert and Wendy KilBride; Aidan Mackey; National Art Library, London and Sally Williams of the Reprographics Dept; National Library of Ireland, Dublin; Ben Panciera, Hesburgh Library, University of Notre Dame, Indiana; Chris. Pedley, SJ, Heythrop College, London; Arthur Rope; Abbot

Geoffrey Scott and monks of Douai Abbey; Tate Gallery library and archives, London; Scott Taylor, Georgetown University Library, Washington DC; Dame Margaret Truran, Stanbrook Abbey; West Yorkshire Archives, Bradford; Dr Michael Williams. I apologize to anyone I have missed out who may have contributed in any way and for any involuntary infringement of copyright that may have occurred.

Especial thanks go to Mgr Philip Moger, now Dean of Leeds Cathedral, for taking time out from his busy schedule to read the manuscript and write the Foreword. Last but not least, I thank my husband, Dr David Smith, for his constant support, encouragement, and indexing skills.

Chapter 1

1870–95: Early Years and Education

The story of Father Brown begins in Clonmel, Ireland, with the birth of John Joseph O'Connor on 5 December 1870. Clonmel lies on the banks of the River Suir in Co. Tipperary but already there is a duality in John Joseph's life, as he was born in Co. Waterford, the county boundary running down the middle of the river. Married the previous March in the Roman Catholic Pro-cathedral in Dublin, his parents Michael O'Connor and Bridget Mulcahy had a further four children, all girls, two of whom died young.

A few months after Michael O'Connor's marriage, an advertisement in the Clonmel Chronicle announced that Michael was re-opening the Spring-Garden dye-works and woollen factory. He had already engaged a first-class staff but lacked a few weavers and a good second-hand pump. As his father, John, had also been a merchant, this could be his factory that is being re-opened after his death which had occurred before Michael's marriage. It went on to say that Michael O'Connor had just finished some heavy friezes, tweeds, flannels, and blankets in various colours and these pure Irish woollen cloths could be inspected at the Warehouse, Old Bridge. This seems to refer to the Irish Tweed and Wool Warehouse, Old Bridge, which, in an earlier advertisement in the same newspaper, announced that M. O'Connor had a new stock of woollen goods in various grades. They were also able to manufacture blankets, tweeds and the like from the customer's own wool and these could be dyed as could

River Suir, Old Bridge and Suir Island area, Clonmel.

clothing, carpets and curtains. Orders were also being taken for gentlemen's tailoring. As an agent for McDougalls sheep and lamb-dipping composition and foot-rot ointment, he was conveniently caring for wool both on and off the sheep. These notices seem to suggest that these are two different factories, one headed by Michael, the other by his father and subsequently taken over by Michael.

This area of Old Bridge and Suir Island boasted a number of factories and warehouses in the 1870s but many of them have either disappeared or have been turned into modern waterside apartments, making it difficult now to trace particular establishments. I was fortunate to have as my guide in Clonmel, Mrs Margaret Rossiter, a well-known local historian, who took me on a walking tour of the area, and who showed me what she thought were a couple of likely candidates for the O'Connor mills. Born into this wealthy wool manufacturing family, John Joseph would subsequently feel at home among the wool manufacturers he would meet in Bradford. Coincidentally, the prices on the Bradford Wool Exchange were quoted in the same Clonmel newspaper as his

A likely candidate for Michael O'Connor's warehouse, Clonmel.

father's advertisements but most of these mills have gone the same way as those in Clonmel.

John Joseph's mother, Bridget Mulcahy, came from a farming family. Her father, John, inherited a piece of untilled land covered with whin bushes but growing tired of trying to wrest a living from this rocky ground, he decided to leave and try his luck elsewhere. He packed his bag intending to walk to Waterford the next day to catch a boat and work his passage to America but during the night he awoke to see a figure standing by his bed. Though she died when he was only three years old, he recognized his mother who told him to stay where he was. Next day he did as he was bid and unpacked his bag.

The land to the south and south-east of Clonmel, lying in County Waterford, was less fertile and more mountainous than that to the north in Tipperary and it was here that John became a tenant farmer on a large estate. One of the joys of the young John Joseph was to be taken by horse and trap into these mountains to his grandfather's farm where the bread and butter were different and tea was made with copious amounts of cream and sugar.

The house was a long, half-thatched one-storey house which was added to as the Mulcahy family grew in numbers and resources. In his unpublished *Mixed Memories*,[1] Father O'Connor recalled a new two-storey farmhouse being built when he was about four years old and it being considered quite a mansion. The centre part of the old house was used to store turf for the fires which added a special smell and cosiness to the house. The 'new parlour' of the old house became a meal and corn store, while the 'old parlour' became the principal piggery with its own small yard surrounded by wild fuchsia.

Grandfather John had almost lost the farm when his family were just babies. As he was walking home from Mass one Sunday, not yet having acquired a trap, he met the estate agent who told him that because he had always been a good tenant he was giving him early warning that he would soon be getting three months' notice to quit in order that the agent's friend could have the farm. In no uncertain terms, farmer John told him that if the agent took his living, he would take the agent's life in what he considered a fair exchange! The agent took the threat seriously and left John to continue his farming in peace.

John Mulcahy was a handsome, wild and fearless man who once literally took a bull by the horns to save a farmhand from being gored to death, but a shake of the fist by his wife would send him meekly to bed if he came home having had a drop too much to drink. Undoubtedly, he was also a good man, kind and compassionate to those less fortunate than himself and when an old priest was being forcibly retired he invited him to stay at the farm. Unfortunately, the Bishop insisted he go to a Home for the Aged outside the parish. John could only provide a flat cart to take him there, so in order to ease the old man's journey, he lay down his best feather bed in it. As he left, the priest sat up and raising his hands to heaven he said, but in his native tongue, 'John, may the blessing of the broken-hearted be always with you!'[2]

During the famine the blessings of the broken-hearted were heaped upon this compassionate farmer. Relief ships were bringing Indian corn into the country but it was not being ground quick enough. In order to speed up the process, Farmer John took one of his farm labourers and, together with the local joiner, built a water mill less than fifty yards down the stream, which ran in front of the house, to grind the corn himself. The meal was used to make huge quantities of porridge which were put outside the gate for famine-stricken travellers to help themselves. It was well known that no man dare beg from him, but those in need didn't need to, for John would get off his horse to give money to the poor beggars sitting by the Convent gates. Poor, out-of-work and sick parishioners had reason to heap similar blessings on his grandson, as Father O'Connor also found many ingenious ways of quietly helping those in need.

John Mulcahy was a literate man who enjoyed buying the weekly newspaper and reading it to his less literate neighbours. In the *Clonmel Chronicle* in May 1870, the same issue in which Michael O'Connor's advertisements appeared, there was a meeting of the Clonmel Farmers Club to discuss the grand jury laws which affected all ratepayers. One John Mulcahy was present at this meeting and, as this was a common name in the area, I cannot be sure this was grandfather John, but it seems the sort of cause he would espouse. The farmers intended submitting a petition after reading the evidence put before the Select Committee of the House of Commons in 1868 on grand jury presentments. The Irish tenant farmers, who contributed ninety-six per cent of the money, were not only not examined or asked for their opinions but were particularly refused. While they alone had a grievance and demanded a voice, the people who were examined were the very ones in whose departments the abuses existed. A report founded on such evidence, they argued, would only tend to strengthen or make little change to the present law. During the 1870s, there was a drive by Irish urban authorities to become fiscally independent of the grand juries and, in 1879, Clonmel Corporation was granted a such an order.

On the night of 5 December 1880, his grandson's tenth birthday, seventy-eight-year-old John Mulcahy drowned in the sea at Dungarvan as he walked to his daughter's house, possibly caught by the tide as he crossed the bay. His wife outlived him by over twenty years, dying aged ninety-seven.

John Joseph O'Connor first realized his existence when he
was almost a year and half and was awakened by his mother
holding his baby hand in hers and remarking to herself how
little it was. When he heard this, the sentence. 'It won't always
be so little'³ formed in his mind. Such sentences often formed
in his mind long before he could speak a word, so twenty years
later when he heard a theory that words produced thoughts, he
knew that, at least for him, thoughts produced words he was
incapable of uttering.

There was no shortage of primary schools in Clonmel, but
John Joseph's early learning was very informal. By the age of
three, he knew his capital letters, 'A' being his particular
favourite, 'S' made him laugh as it reminded him of the fat
ducks on his grandmother's pond and 'R' was his enemy as he
was unable to pronounce it until an uncle with keen views on
elocution boxed both his ears simultaneously and he was
frightened into it. Able to read before he was five years old, a
great deal seems to have been self-taught as he wandered
around the garden with occasional reference to a grown-up.
Growing up in beautiful surroundings on the slopes of
Scouthea, looking over the valley to Slievenamon, he had an
intuitive love of natural beauty for it is only in his second
reading book that he recalls being almost moved to tears by the
lines 'The glorious sun has set in the west. The night dew falls.
The air which was sultry becomes cool; the flowers fold up
their coloured leaves and hang their heads on slender stalks.'⁴
The words had added emphasis for him as he was walking in
the garden with his book at about the time of a glorious sunset
and together they filled him with a 'choking melancholy'⁵ that
made him 'home-sick for beauty'.⁶

Father O'Connor remembered his schooldays at the St Francis
Academy as being 'the most miserable and degrading waste of
time it has ever been my lot to experience'.⁷ The school had
opened on Mary Street on 1 September 1873 in response to the
demand for second-level education. John Joseph's misery began
when he was six years old, just after Easter 1877. Lessons
started at 9 a.m. and finished at 3 p.m., with a half-hour break
for lunch. Catechism, spelling and writing took up the morning

with drawing, geography and arithmetic in the afternoon. Older students were coached for the Intermediate examination. John's early home tuition in arithmetic had ended in tears so was left until school where it was overshadowed by the awfulness of learning to write. The young scholar never managed to hold the pen right, the needle-sharp points went through the paper, and being rapped over the knuckles did nothing at all to improve his handwriting. He was more impressed by the saintly headmaster who was the only priest in Ireland ever to give him religious instruction, and one of the few anywhere who made it really interesting. This same headmaster, in a less saintly moment, gave the young John the best caning he ever had but it was for bad language, of which he heard more at that school than the poor school he went to next. The caning didn't have the desired effect as Father O'Connor's propensity for swearing was well-known throughout his life. Few of the friars were interested in teaching and pupil numbers fell as the parents refused to continue paying the school fees and the school closed in July 1881.

John O'Connor may have considered his days with the Franciscans a waste of time but the following two years with the Irish Christian Brothers more than made up for them. School work and vast amounts of homework made learning an almost continuous process as the pupils worked towards the Intermediate examinations; results fees from these were what the school depended on. After John Joseph had taken the Intermediate examination, winning a prize of books to the value of three pounds, it was decided that he, like the sons of many wealthy Catholics of the time, would be sent abroad to complete his education.

In August 1883, the twelve-year-old John Joseph O'Connor left his beloved green hills of Waterford to sail to Milford Haven in Wales, the first leg of his journey to the Benedictines of Douai in Flanders. Though he often visited relatives remaining in Ireland, he was never to live there again. Through a mistake on the part of his elders, John Joseph arrived in London a week too soon to meet to the rest of the boys who were to travel on to Douai together. Whether a grown-up took him as far as Calais

Douai school photograph, 1883. John O'Connor, second from left.

we don't know, but he did travel alone on the night train from Calais then slept in the waiting room at Lille as he waited for the six o'clock train to Douai, where he arrived just in time for the morning Mass of the Assumption. He later recalled with fondness, the graciousness and cordiality with which he was received by the Sub-Prior, Father Norbert Ward, for he was 'very small and lonesome'.[8] Every night for six weeks the homesick little boy cried himself to sleep, and tried to wake up before the other boys so he could weep in private.

John Joseph worked hard, and after the strain of examinations, Christmas was a time for relaxation and Christmas celebrations at Douai were something to write home about. John's parents were probably surprised at the news that their young son was smothered in muslin as he sewed 'millions' of spangles on the fairies' costumes for a production of *Iolanthe*. As assistant to a future Canon and Vicar General of Southwark, in a production in which a future Bishop of Lancaster made an excellent Fairy Queen, he was in good company.

Midnight Mass was followed by a Low Mass of Thanksgiving and a visit to the Crib with its life-size figures, before the Head Prefect brought in the letters of the past week.

Christmas Dinner was veal and beefsteak, plum pudding and white sauce stirred with the cork from a brandy bottle, followed by two glasses of the finest Bordeaux and three jam turnovers. Religious and secular occupations existed happily side by side, as did pupils and monks. Christmas night Vespers were followed by *vingt-et-un* played for butter beans bought from the Prefect at one sou for twenty. At the end of the vacation, any remaining beans could be sold back to the Prefect. Monks who could stand the noise in the playrooms would join the boys in their games; one such was Father Norbert Ward who came every day to play whist. He was over eighteen stone and took no offence when he discovered a banner in the Seniors' Room declaring : VIVAT FAT[R] SUBPRIOR.[9]

The new prior, Charles Oswald O'Neill, arrived on 27 December, and in his honour Father Christmas was solemnly carried in. The latter was Captain of the School and his make-up served for his title role in *King Lear* which followed the pageant. The following morning the young boys took to the stage to perform a rhyming burlesque of *Alfred and the Cakes*; John O'Connor played Mrs Smith, the baker's wife. The production of *Iolanthe* brought the festivities of that first Christmas at Douai to an end. Everyone alike working hard to amuse themselves and making the most of what little they had, had made it an exciting event which left no time at all for homesickness.

It was not until about the age of sixteen that the future Monsignor John O'Connor became, as he himself phrased it, 'God-conscious'.[10] Public worship, private devotions and the daily example of the monastic and dedicated lives of the Benedictines had their effect on the young man. However, if there were no Church, Bible or Saints, he felt he would still be a 'Vessel of Revelation',[11] and there were many days when he felt he 'walked in heaven'.[12] He had long ago learned the Apostles' Creed in Ireland but remembered kneeling on a kitchen chair to repeat it, all the while facing the kitchen clock which, as he later admits, he mistakenly personified as God.

An early representation of God was a Bartolozzi engraving at

the end of his bed at home, but the face that gazed heavenward
left less impression on the boy's mind than the sight of his father
looking upwards as he knelt at his morning prayers. Walking to
Mass with his father by the clear waters of the River Suir, where
salmon gathered in season, with the rooks cawing in the elms and
the friary bell ringing, left the boy in a kind of rapture. His
grandfather's habit of saying the Rosary as he rode home on his
horse, and again with the family after supper, left a lasting
impression, as his future parishioners recalled their parish priest
'telling his beads' whenever he was out walking alone.

Even the best-intentioned little boys, however, can be
tempted and young John was no exception. One day the
eight-year-old was unable to resist the temptation to take away
and keep an ivory-topped pencil but, as it was never missed,
there was never any trouble about it but the young boy was
sorely troubled about what he had done. Later he admitted he
never felt that God was at all interested in his trouble, he only
felt he had fallen below his own perfect standard. After his
terrible torments, the ivory top turned out to be bone!

Formal religious education did little to inspire the young John
and it was no thanks to his early tutors that he ever cared
anything about what he was taught. Having to learn five different
catechisms had stimulated no religious fervour, but reading for
himself the words of God in the Sunday Gospels stayed with him
all his life. His faith grew rather from his natural striving for
perfection, as in the case of the purloined pencil, from his
response to the natural beauty of sunsets, sparkling rivers, and
green, rolling hills, and from the perfect happiness which filled
his soul as he listened to beautiful music.

It was at Douai, in particular in Sunday Vespers sung in
Latin, that his sensitive soul approached ecstasy. It was here
too that he had to learn *The Dream of Gerontius* for a Speech
Day. Written in 1865, by John Henry Newman who had
converted to Catholicism twenty years earlier, it is a vision of
a just soul leaving the body at death; John had to learn the
Guardian Angel's great soliloquy. The piece made a mighty
impression on him for he began to pray every day at the
Elevation in the Mass, that one day it would be set to music.

Edward Elgar duly obliged and some twelve years later Father O'Connor heard the composer himself conduct the oratorio in Worcester Cathedral, but kept to himself the secret bond he had with Elgar.

Though terribly homesick as the young John O'Connor was when he first arrived in Douai, he, like many others before and after him, experienced a homesickness for the school when he left. This was due more to the sense of brotherhood the boys shared with the monks than the comfort of their accommodation or the quality of their studies. Many years later Father O'Connor found himself giving the vote of thanks to the headmaster of Ampleforth College, for a paper to the Newman Society on the Benedictine System and finding it so similar to his own experience of Douai. 'The Holy Spirit who invented growth must inspire for ever the Benedictine way of life', he said, 'even for the boys who feel the soreness of the price they have to pay, but only after long years esteem the value of their purchase.'[13]

In 1903, anti-clerical laws caused the Benedictines to be expelled from Douai. They moved to England and established a 'new' Douai Abbey in Woolhampton, Berkshire. Father O'Connor was a guest when the foundation stone of the new Abbey Church was laid in June1928, and again in June 1933 when the east end of the church was opened. In February 2006, a new priory, the Maison St Benoît, re-established the presence of the Benedictine monks of St Edmund's in Douai, a very happy event for all past and present Dowegians.

Over the years, he donated many paintings to the Abbey. He also gifted one of the very few copies ever made of the Ardagh Chalice, one of the finest examples of Celtic art to be found and now in the National Museum of Ireland. It is said that Queen Elizabeth, mother of Queen Elizabeth II, had tried, and failed, to obtain this copy, which was left by Father O'Connor to a fellow Dowegian, on the condition that he left it to Douai Abbey.

Father O'Connor regularly visited Woolhampton and was an active Old Dowegian, being some time President of the Douai Society. After one Douai Society meeting, a group of them carried on to Rome for a meeting of the Roman Association, an association of past students of the Venerable English College of which Father O'Connor was also an active member. Towards the end of the nineteenth century, there was a dire shortage of priests in England and many Old Dowegians went on to Rome to continue their studies at the Venerable English College. John was awarded one of the places allocated to the Diocese of Leeds, where two of his mother's brothers already were.

After a short holiday in Clonmel, in October 1889 John O'Connor once more set sail from Waterford harbour, this time on a cattle boat bound for Liverpool en route to Rome. The few passengers included two of his sisters, the eldest, seventeen-year-old Mary Margaret was bound for Belgium where she was to join the Sisters of Notre Dame de Namur, while their eight-year-old youngest sister was to join a boarding school of the same Order in England. As John left Mary Margaret at the convent, he experienced his last dose of home sickness on the train taking him to Douai where he was greeted with a warm welcome from old friends.

From Douai he and a friend travelled on by train to Rome, via Paris, where they visited the Paris Exhibition and 'listened to the music in the wind in the girders'[14] of the newly built Eiffel Tower. Coming out they were caught in a thunderstorm but the sun emerging from the black clouds lit the Cathedral of Notre Dame in a blaze of colour. John slept during the journey through the Alps, awakening to his first sight of the great cathedral of Milan. The boys spent a morning on the roof of the cathedral and thought it one of the wonders of the world until, on a later visit, they saw the golden altar at St Ambrogio. Last stop on this brief tour of Europe was Florence, where the boys made the stiff uphill climb to San Miniato al Monte from where they had a sensational view of the city, though by this time they had been overcome with fatigue. They stayed at the convent of the Little Company of Mary whose Sisters devote themselves to the sick and dying of any nationality or creed. One of their number had been sent to Venice to nurse Robert Browning in his last illness. They talked with the Foundress, Mary Hunter, on many subjects but were most impressed by an indefinable and thrilling aura which seemed to emanate from her. Leaving Florence behind, the boys finally arrived in Rome in the grey of an October dawn.

Father O'Connor felt he could never thank God enough for his studies in Rome, arduous as they had been, but his *Mixed Memories* tell us little about them. The official archives at the college show only a dry list of dates of when he achieved minor orders, steps on the way to his eventual ordination as priest in 1895. A little more light is shed on the subject by a tale I was told by Father Thomas Keegan, one-time curate to Father O'Connor. An elderly lady told him how, when she was just a young woman, she had travelled through Europe with her father and sister and when in Rome they had called on the Rector of the English College. Knowing they were from the Leeds diocese, he told them that at present they had two students from the diocese in the college, both of them were clever but one of them was brilliant. The two students were Arthur Hinsley, who became Rector of the college in 1917 until 1930, and Cardinal of Westminster in 1935, and John O'Connor. It was the latter who was the brilliant one. Cardinal Heenan, in his biography of Cardinal Hinsley, wrote that 'The very variety of life in Rome and the emphasis of Roman studies which are directed to the formation of future professors rather than pastors, necessarily leave the Roman student in some directions less well equipped than others for life on the mission.'[15] John O'Connor managed to be well-equipped in both directions.

The Venerable English College, or Venerabile as it was affectionately known, was the second oldest college affiliated to the Gregorian University and, as such, the students held a place of honour in the lecture hall. Here they came into contact with students from many other nations as they studied philosophy, theology and canon law. They were considered a conscientious group who could be trusted never to waste their time, which was more than could be said of some of their professors, recalled Father O'Connor.

The Vice-Rector of the English College was Monsignor John Prior, whom John O'Connor first met when he was a young pupil spending his first summer holiday in Douai. Fathers John Prior and Joseph Cowgill, both old Dowegians and newly ordained Romans visited the college and had the boys, unwillingly, perform their parlour-tricks. The 'lively inattention'[16] of Father Cowgill, later his bishop in Leeds, contrasted with the 'stern and deadly attention'[17] of Father Prior, under whose scrutiny he would so often come, when they met again in Rome. Initially afraid of him, John O'Connor eventually came to call John Prior 'the friend of my soul',[18] as he felt able to say to him, more than to any other person, whatever was in his mind.

Summer vacations were spent at the Villa Inglese, among the vineyards of Monte Porzio Catone in the Alban hills, south-east of Rome. When Doctor Prior's piano arrived there from England, he initiated musical afternoons. Not only did the good doctor introduce the students to Beethoven, Schubert and string quartets, he also provided them, at his own expense, with cakes and wine, no doubt equally appreciated.

The Rector of the Venerabile was Doctor William Giles, 'a scholar, gentleman and saint with the heart of a child' who 'nevertheless contrived to make himself infinitely absurd on nearly all occasions'.[19] There was never a student who failed to rag him in some way or other, and Father O'Connor regretted the times he himself must have wounded the Rector and tried him beyond the limit. Indeed, he felt that it was likely that he only escaped dire punishment through the intervention of Doctor Prior, though he could be trying also to him. Doctor Giles always planned the students' visits, being conversant with bus and train timetables and the qualities of hostelries, and paid expenses, the English College being in straightened circumstances.

Doctor Giles could be tough when necessary and fought a long campaign to ensure that priests were ordained before the end of the course. He frowned on those college boys who felt it necessary to return to England during the summer holidays, for as a rule they would return home only once during the whole of their student years. Studies continued each morning during the holidays and students were encouraged to see their professors after lectures either in Rome or away in the countryside, wrangling with them about anything they chose. Learning was virtually a continuous process throughout the whole of the course.

Summer holidays ended with a ten days' Retreat, with a supply of chocolate and biscuits for each boy, courtesy of Doctor Giles. Retreats, in Father O'Connor's experience, left one with a fearful hunger and insatiable thirst, and at the end of a perfect day came a peaceful sleep, leading him to conclude that 'a vigorous spiritual life is life abounding'.[20] This he discovered first at Douai where, as at all Benedictine establishments, silence was imposed from night prayers until after breakfast. Though he found it irksome and unreasonable as a small boy, he later found it gave one a 'preternatural concentration and fertility of mind'.[21] However, the 'rigid righteousness'[22] of these retreats led, by about the ninth day, to serious divinity students being seized with the giggles and turning cartwheels in the corridors.

Intense as the academic studies were, they were not the only means by which students at the Venerabile were educated, for the Eternal City herself played her part as the boys discovered her ancient monuments and attended ceremonial occasions. On their first Sunday in Rome, in November 1889, they went to the Hall of Canonization for the beatification of St John Gabriel Perboyre by Pope Leo XIII. He was crucified on Good Friday, 1840, and in June 1996 was canonized and declared a saint by Pope John Paul II.

The catacombs of ancient Rome were to become very familiar to John O'Connor and his fellow students as they became expert guides, entrusted with leading English groups around them. After spending one afternoon underground, John found himself quite in favour of cremation, long before it received the approval of the Church, as he discovered that, after fifteen hundred years, internment produced the same piles of grey ash as a cremated body produced in a matter of hours.

Annually, on 31 December, the students went to the Catacomb of Priscilla for the feast of St Sylvester. The catacomb, the oldest of the Christian cemeteries, was of particular interest for its close connection with Peter and Paul. Sepulchral slabs bore the names 'Peter' and 'Paul', proof that the corpse was baptized by one or the other because of the ancient custom of the baptized taking the name of their spiritual father. A decorated pool on the last floor is traditionally that in which Peter carried out baptisms.

Frequent visits were made to the surrounding towns and villages and their history soaked up. During the summer months every village held its feast when bells rang, shots were let off and the village bands played. In Monte Porzio Catone the students assisted at the High Mass before taking part in the grand procession around the village. A towering framework of fire crackers was let off, and on one occasion, as young John led the procession he was concussed by the first of them. The day continued with another church service and more music before the big event, the sending up of the Fire Balloon. These mini hot-air balloons made of paper were fired up into the night sky, unfortunately it was not unknown for them to burst into flames and set fire to whatever they landed upon. On at least one occasion the boys found themselves having to dash for buckets of water as their hedge caught fire, no rain for months having made the whole countryside highly inflammable.

Living in Rome, the students at the Venerabile benefited not only from being able to visit historic towns and villages, but also from the people who visited the Venerabile, as Father O'Connor said 'everyone that was anyone used to turn up there at some time or other'.[23] Visiting cards were left and their card tray was soon piled high, each having to be duly exchanged in person or by sending a manservant. A Night of Stars and Garters[24] was how Father O'Connor described one reception at the English College, where he saw all the rarest and most coveted Orders of Chivalry in the world, worn by some of the most distinguished personages in Europe. But it was the devotion of the ordinary Roman people who attended the special celebrations that took place at the shrines around the city throughout the year that he most admired. Already, as a young student, he had his feet firmly on the ground, unimpressed by grandeur and status he took people as they were, not according to who they were.

After six years of intensive study, sojourns in the Italian countryside, festivals and receptions, John O'Connor was ordained priest in March 1895. The ordination took place in the Basilica of St John Lateran by Archbishop, the Most Revd Hon. Edmund Stonor. Father O'Connor, assisted by Doctor Prior, said his first Mass on the tomb of St Peter. In those days only a cardinal or member of the chapter could procure admission to the crypt of St Peter's as various attempts had been made to blow it up. He was fortunate that at this time the Archbishop of Westminster, Cardinal Vaughan, was staying at the English College and was able to obtain the necessary permission. It was after this Mass that Father O'Connor had his only psychic experience which he described 'as the nostalgia for the Infinite',[25] a piercing sadness that filled him as he came back down to earth. Despite the excitement of going home and starting work in a parish, it was two years before this sense of melancholy left him.

Notes
1. O'Connor, *Father Brown's Mixed Memories*.
2. Ibid.
3. Ibid.
4. O'Connor, 'The Infancy of Father Brown', *The Sower*, pp. 319–21.
5. Ibid.
6. O'Connor, *Father Brown's Mixed Memories*.
7. Ibid.
8. O'Connor, 'Some Pressed Flowers from Old Douai', *The Douai Magazine*, pp. 297–9.
9. O'Connor, 'Christmas 1883', *The Douai Magazine*, pp. 379–84.
10. O'Connor, *Father Brown's Mixed Memories*.
11. Ibid.
12. Ibid.
13. O'Connor, 'Old Douai', *The Douai Magazine*, pp. 8–12.
14. O'Connor, *Father Brown's Mixed Memories*.
15. Heenan, *Cardinal Hinsley*, p. 24.
16. Redmond, 'Monsignor John Prior', *The Venerabile*, pp. 5–16.
17. Ibid.
18. Ibid.
19. O'Connor, *Father Brown's Mixed Memories*.
20. Ibid.

21. Ibid.
22. Ibid.
23. Ibid.
24. Ibid.
25. Ibid.

Chapter 2

1895–1902: Church and School, Music and Literature

After a brief visit to his Irish homeland, Father O'Connor crossed the water to England yet again, this time to take up his priestly duties within the Diocese of Leeds, where, apart from holidays, he stayed for the rest of his life. This, however, in no way restricted his becoming a well-known and respected member of artistic and literary circles both in this country and abroad. 'A dazzling conversationalist; a great diner-out and lover of good food – fine wine and cigars ... He was a connoisseur in the art of living, just as he was in the world of politics, music and books', was how Yorkshire author and St Cuthbert's parishioner, Alfred J. Brown , described him.[1]

The Diocese of Leeds was established while John Joseph was still a schoolboy in Ireland in 1878, and comprised the whole of the West Riding of Yorkshire. Before local government re-organization in the 1970s, the county reputedly had more acres than letters in the Bible and was divided into three Ridings, West, North and East, with the West, covering 2,775 square miles, being the largest. The Diocesan Cathedral Church of St Anne in Leeds, described as the best Catholic Cathedral in the country outside Westminster, was not completed until some nine years after Father O'Connor arrived in nearby Bradford. Close to pretty Dales villages and on the edge of the moors which inspired the writings of the famous Brontë sisters, the new priest found himself in one of the less attractive areas of this industrial town, which was granted city status two years later.

The population of Bradford in 1801 was just under 14,000; by the beginning of the next century it had risen to over 200,000. This was mainly due to the influx of two very different types of migrant, both of which would feature largely in Father O'Connor's life. Many poverty-stricken Irish found themselves seeking work in the large textile mills, and as most of them were Catholics, some would find themselves his eventual parishioners, their spiritual welfare in his very capable hands.

The second group to make their homes in Bradford in the mid nineteenth century were wealthy merchants of German-Jewish origin, thus their connection to a Roman Catholic priest not being immediately obvious, indeed being somewhat unusual perhaps. Part of Bradford's heritage is an area of huge Italianate warehouses built by these merchants and still known as 'Little Germany'. With their international links they helped to establish Bradford as the centre of the world's wool trade, but not all the sons of these merchants wished to enter their fathers' businesses; many were more concerned with art or music. One famous son was the composer Frederick Delius, whose father, Julius, had started trading in Bradford in 1850, but it was art and literature that brought Father O'Connor into contact with these German immigrants, especially members of the Rothenstein and Steinthal families, of whom more later.

In 1822, a priest was sent from Leeds to minister to the Bradford Catholics, who had previously had to walk to Leeds to hear Mass. The first Mass to be celebrated in Bradford since the Reformation took place, despite opposition, in a hired room at the Roebuck Inn. Further opposition led to another move but in 1825 a site was acquired for the first St Mary's church. When the Catholic Emancipation Act of 1829 allowed Catholics to worship openly and as the Catholic population increased, further churches were built. St Joseph's, where Father John O'Connor first practised his ministry, started life as a school-chapel in 1868 but in 1887 a fine new church, accommodating 800 worshippers, was opened in Pakington Street, where it still stands today. A new school-chapel, dedicated to St Cuthbert followed ten years later, catering for the

Manningham district of the town. In 1891 this was also replaced by a new church and presbytery on Wilmer Road, overlooking the Heaton reservoir, where Monsignor John O'Connor would end his ministry.

When Father O'Connor came as new curate to join Canon Motler, parish priest of St Joseph's church in 1895, he thought

St Joseph's church, Bradford; Fr O'Connor's first posting as curate.

that he had never come across a livelier or better set of people. He encountered a rather different set of people in the Poor Law Union Workhouse, just minutes away from his grand church, and what he saw there and in the surrounding back streets, where conditions made those of even the workhouse seem like paradise, could hardly be more of a contrast to his life in Rome. It was here that he would encounter many of the atrocities, and much of the wickedness and evil, the knowledge of which would astound his, as yet unknown, friend G. K. Chesterton and inspire him to create his priest-detective Father Brown.

The 1834 Poor Law Amendment Act required people receiving help from the parish to live and work in the workhouse and enabled parishes to form unions responsible for their building and running. The new Bradford workhouse had been built in 1852 in Little Horton Lane and was known locally as 'Horton College'. The 'college' inhabitants were the poverty-stricken, the orphaned, poor widows and tramps, the sick and the deranged. With some 470 beds, the place was overcrowded, while poor diet meant that illness and disease were rife. There was no trained nurse to minister to the sick until 1896 when two trained nurses came, but they soon left as they complained it was impossible to obtain even a piece of sterilized cotton wool with which to dress horrific wounds. Fortunately, the situation improved a few years later when a Nurses' Home was built and a matron and her staff moved in.

A family entering the workhouse would find themselves split up; men, women, children, the elderly and the infirm being housed separately after being stripped, searched and washed. They were given a uniform to wear, basic food to eat and a dormitory in which to sleep. Able-bodied residents were given hard work to do, while the infirm would be cared for in hospital wards. 'Bradforditis' referred to the smell of the hospital and Father O'Connor found himself fortunately immune to it, as he was to typhus and smallpox, both of which he came in contact with on more than one occasion.

Boys and girls had to have three hours a day instruction in reading, writing and the Christian religion, intended to impart to them the habits of usefulness, industry and virtue. Canon Motler, Father O'Connor's parish priest, was employed to instruct them in religious knowledge, both Roman Catholic and Nonconformist. Young girls who had not acquired a virtuous habit could find themselves inside the workhouse as unmarried mothers. 'An Angel of Light'[2] was how Father O'Connor described Nurse Storey, who had charge of the ward, and acted as mother and father-confessor to the unfortunate girls in her care. Though not a Catholic herself, when the priest was called to give the Last Rites to young girls dying of syphilis, she would have flowers and candles ready on a white cloth. It was in Nurse Storey's care that Father O'Connor discovered the daughter of a parish family, who finding herself pregnant had disappeared without their knowledge. This case eventually led to a Rescue Society being set up, funded by a monthly collection in the parish, to help girls in similar circumstances.

By late afternoon tramps would begin to gather outside the Casual Ward, where they hoped to be given a meal and a bed for the night, but some 'Old Stagers' used to wait until after nine o'clock, when the ward door was locked, to gain admittance to the church for the night. Thomas Steele, the tramp-master, said this was preferred by tramps with children as, in order to give the children a badly needed rest, Thomas, and his wife Sarah, would keep them there another night. Sometimes the children were not even the tramps' own, but were being used to add poignancy to their begging.

A further class of workhouse inmates were the lunatics, imbeciles and idiots, some of whom Father O'Connor met again when, as assistant chaplain, he visited Armley Prison, situated between Leeds and Bradford. On one of his visits to the workhouse, a young woman in a padded room glared right through him, 'like frozen lightning'.[3] He found himself subjected to this same glare, which again turned his knees to jelly, when on his rounds of the prison, the woman having been charged with 'Obscene language and solicitation' in Manningham Lane, Bradford.

The area around Manchester Road, in which St Joseph's was situated, was inhabited by the 'poorest of the poor',[4] the woolcombers. The process of 'combing' the wool produced a worsted material which earned Bradford the nickname of Worstedopolis. The mills ran day and night and it was not unknown for the mother in the family to work all day and the father all night, often in temperatures of eighty-four degrees. A decent, hard-working couple, of Father O'Connor's acquaintance, met outside the mill at six o'clock in the evening as the father, coming on the night shift, handed over the baby to the mother finishing her day shift.

One of Father O'Connor's parishioners, Bartle, was very poor and very old, reduced to living in a cellar-kitchen, under houses just as dirty and almost as poor, a terrible place in which not even the worst criminal would be placed, unless as a punishment. Being dirty himself and on crutches, he had been quickly removed from St Joseph's church on his last visit for spoiling the marble pavement, but the young curate regarded him as the 'only lovely thing in a very unlovely building'[5] and took Holy Communion to him in his hovel. The last time Father O'Connor saw Bartle was on Easter Sunday 1898, a horrible morning almost as dark outside as in, but the old man had managed to drag himself up on to a table under a window so he had enough light to read the Gospel of St John in his old sixpenny New Testament.

On another occasion, when Father O'Connor was called to administer to a dying man he had difficulty in finding him as the room was almost as dark as the cellar below, lit as it was by only a street light. As he felt his way carefully around he came across a heap of black rags lying on the worm-eaten floor; on closer inspection the heap of rags were revealed as his parishioner. All life was here in these mean streets, peopled by characters with whom Dickens would have felt familiar, but there was always at least one good and charitable family who had the respect of the even the worst of them.

The young curate was known not only to those of his own faith, but to those of other faiths or even none at all. A particular friend was a wild, heathen mechanic who enjoyed a game of draughts with the priest, beating him every time. On one occasion during the game, the man and his wife disputed the degrees of intimacy which she allowed the lodger! This perhaps prepared him for a similar situation revealed many years later by his friend, the sculptor and engraver Eric Gill.

In 1898, Father O'Connor left behind the mills and unsavoury streets of Bradford but moved only a few miles away to another West Riding mill town, to be curate to his uncle, Father, later Canon, Pat Mulcahy. Halifax produced woollens and worsteds in its mills but was especially famous for carpet manufacture. It was also famous, or infamous, until 1650, for cutting off the heads of cloth-stealers and other criminals. The Church of St Marie stands in Gibbet Street but the gibbet itself was long gone when Father O'Connor arrived to take up his duties.

In December of the same year, a circular arrived at St Marie's which had some rather surprising results and a long-lasting effect on the newly arrived curate. The circular requested hints which might be useful in the compilation of the *Arundel Hymns,* but for Father O'Connor it brought profound and lasting friendships with national politicians and statesmen and membership of an élite literary club. But not yet.

The Arundel Hymns, the first part of which had already been published, was being edited by Henry, Duke of Norfolk and Charles Tindal Gatty, and it was from the latter the circular had come. Father O'Connor's reply[6] expressed his delight with the idea and, though he was unable to offer any hints, he could offer three contributions if Gatty so wished. Father O'Connor himself had long had the idea of a hymnal, so he was delighted when he received a reply from Gatty indicating that his help would be appreciated. He immediately sent off copies of translations he had made from Latin, and made suggestions as to whom Gatty should contact for further advice on the choice of hymns and their settings. His input was duly acknowledged in part two with the editors' thanks, not only for the great service he had brought to the project through his exceptional gifts, but for his sympathy with the whole work.

Charles Gatty sent Father O'Connor the manuscript of part one of the hymnal and he must have discussed this with his fellow priest, Father Downes, as he enclosed the latter's criticism in a letter sent to Gatty in February.[7] The Revd James Francis

Downes was a curate at St Patrick's church, Bradford, and a well-known and respected composer. He had written and composed a Mystery Play in 1894, *The Childhood of Christ,* which concluded with a grand tableau representing the Kingship of the Infant Christ. It was acted by children, though not a play for children, but Father O'Connor thought that the magnificent chorale which accompanied the tableau, though sung with splendid spirit and in unison, was like listening to Handel's *Largo* on a tin whistle and really required three hundred male voices. Father Downes produced a second Mystery Play in 1896 which was seen by over 10,000 people, Protestant as well as Catholic, from a wide area. He wrote part-songs, cantatas and an operetta entitled *A Simple Sweep* and conducted the one-hundred-strong Bradford Catholic Chorale.

After their first meeting, in the spring of 1899, Father O'Connor and Charles Gatty expressed their mutual delight. The latter had visited St Patrick's and, together with Father Downes, who had his own piano there, the three of them had a lengthy discussion about suitable words and music for the hymns. With this first meeting the relationship between Charles Gatty and Father O'Connor took on a new dimension with the beginnings of a real friendship and the start of a long corres-pondence. As his *Mixed Memories* don't comment on his move to Halifax, Father O'Connor's letters to Gatty help shed light on the next few years.

In May, Father O'Connor took to his bed with an unspecified illness, which must have been quite severe as he had to miss Mass for quite some time, something he had not done since his ordination. Although few places were more bracing than Halifax, the invalid felt a change was required but cared neither for the popular northern seaside resort of Scarborough on Yorkshire's east coast or Blackpool on Lancashire's west, there being nothing and nobody at either place to interest him. What did interest him was good company, which was as necessary to him as bracing air, and as Charles Gatty's company was very good, Father O'Connor decided to consult his doctor and seriously consider accepting Gatty's invitation to visit.

The visit did take place but the return journey had tired

Father O'Connor more than he had expected. A short convalescence soon had him back to normal so by the end of June he was well enough to accompany Father Downes to Bayreuth for the performance of Wagner's *Ring Cycle*. Here Father O'Connor was sure they had been sitting next to Gabriele d' Annunzio, the Italian novelist, dramatist and poet, whose works he had been reading only recently. Charles Gatty had also been at Bayreuth but stayed on when the priests returned home. He visited Father O'Connor at Halifax shortly after his return and during his stay they enjoyed a pleasant walk to Shibden Hall to visit John Lister, a founder member of the Independent Labour Party.

In September 1899, Father O'Connor moved to West Vale, on the outskirts of Halifax, to try to establish a separate mission. At that time West Vale had nothing, no church and an income from all sources of only about two pounds a week. Father O'Connor hoped it would grow, but it didn't and he found himself returned to St Marie's after just a few months. However, another possible move was looming on the horizon. A new grammar school was being started in Bradford and Father O'Connor thought, and hoped, he might be asked to take a class. He told his friend that he would be willing to do whatever he could to make it a success, especially in the beginning.

In 1900, permission had just been granted for Catholics to attend non-Catholic universities which opened the way for higher Catholic education. On 12 June Houghton House, Drewton Street, the new St Bede's Grammar School, opened its doors to thirty-seven students, some of whom were boarders accommodated over St Patrick's preparatory school. By September there were sixty students from a variety of social backgrounds. The Revd Dr Hinsley, who had been ordained two years ahead of John O'Connor in Rome, was appointed headmaster and Father O'Connor was appointed as his assistant. At first Father O'Connor lodged at St Patrick's presbytery and there appears to have been some problem about his accommodation, mainly to do with lack of funds on the part of the school governors. Eventually it was all cleared up and he

moved to Camden Terrace. His assistant schoolmaster's salary
was seventy pounds a year, thirty of which went on keep, and
he told Gatty that he only did the job because of his conviction
that 'the Glory of God is bound up with the secondary
education of Catholics'. [8] He got through this trying time by
hearing Elgar conduct his own music in Bradford, which he
described as an 'incomparable intellectual treat'.[9]

Father O'Connor was immensely satisfied in having
achieved whatever Charles Gatty required of him in regard to
the hymnal: twelve original hymns and thirteen translations for
the 1902 edition. While his twenty-year-long pastime of
reading poetry and listening to music had helped him in these
achievements to an extent of which he never thought himself
capable, writing the rhymes had fulfilled a longing within him
to express words which had dogged his adolescent years and at
times had threatened to choke him. He was sure he had to thank
Gatty for much more than Gatty had to thank him. Father
O'Connor ended this letter,[10] as he did so many, with down-
right practical advice for his correspondent, in this case he
advised Gatty to take ammoniated quinine as a cure for
influenza, as it had cured himself three times as if by magic.

Charles Gatty, a convert to Roman Catholicism, was born in
Ecclesfield, near Sheffield in Yorkshire, where his father was
the Anglican vicar. Apart from his work as a hymnologist, he
had a varied career which included museum curator and
newspaper editor. In the summer of 1889, Gatty met George
Wyndham at Derwent Hall, near Sheffield , the home of Lord
Edmund Talbot, second son of the fourteenth Duke of Norfolk,
and brother of the joint editor of the *Arundel Hymns*. George
Wyndham and Charles Gatty immediately became firm friends,
despite their being of different religious and political persua-
sions, as they had shared tastes in the arts. Derwent Hall was
demolished in 1945, its remains now lying under the
Ladybower reservoir.

George Wyndham was a Conservative Member of
Parliament who had married Sibell, Countess Grosvenor,
widowed daughter-in-law of the first Duke of Westminster. In
1901, he was Chief Secretary of Ireland and member of the

Irish Privy Council, his official residence then being the Chief Secretary's Lodge in Phoenix Park, Dublin. In a letter to his mother on 8 August,[11] Wyndham mentioned that they had enjoyed some really good music, with Charles Gatty playing accompaniments and had a poet called O'Connor, but both of them had left that day bound for Suffolk. Charles Gatty had insisted Father O'Connor go with him to Beach House, Felixstowe, the summer home of his friend Robert Hudson, as one of his greatest pleasures was in introducing new friends to old friends from the worlds of politics, literature and music. Of the many friends Gatty had introduced to Robert Hudson, it was for this meeting with the little Irish cleric that Hudson was most grateful.

Robert Hudson was a political organizer, a Liberal who, after their success in 1906, was knighted and Gatty, CTG as he often called him, was his intimate friend. J. A. Spender's memoir of Robert Hudson[12] includes an account of their first meeting, written by Father O'Connor who was much taken with Hudson's welcoming smile. He immediately took the man himself to his heart at the start of what proved to be a long and ideal friendship.

It was a glorious August and Robert, who was a widower, had brought his young daughter and all her friends to Beach House. When the young ones were swimming in the sea, Father O'Connor, apparently a good swimmer, found himself deputed to swim backwards and forwards between them and the deeper water in the interest of safety. Later they all went sailing, bought lobsters on the way home and chanted incantations to amazing orange sunsets which so impressed Father O' Connor that he forever associated lobster with sunsets.

Father O'Connor's love of good company and conversation was amply fulfilled in the evenings as he sat with the 'merry bachelors',[13] as he called them, indulging their passion for music and literature, during which *The Wallet of Kai Lung* was discovered and the Kai Lung Club came into being. Published in 1900, the book was the first novel of Ernest Bramah and introduced Kai Lung, a Chinese teller of tales of adventure. It was not the stories themselves, but rather the way in which they

were written, that attracted the select group who began writing
to each other in their extraordinary style. Ordinary proverbs
and commonplace episodes were so couched in the Chinese
literary manner that it could take a whole afternoon's
concentration to unravel them. Father O'Connor gives an
example in *Father Brown on Chesterton*[14] 'Beware lest when
about to embrace the sublime Emperor, you tread upon the
elusive banana-peel' would eventually be revealed as 'There's
many a slip 'twixt the cup and the lip.' Robert Hudson was the
prime instigator of the club, with Charles Gatty, Father
O'Connor and the author, Bramah, whose real surname was
Smith and who was a near neighbour. Ex-Prime Minister, and
member of the House of Lords, Lord Rosebery and Augustine
Birrell, politician and man of letters were further recruits, as
was Chesterton. The latter inscribed Father O'Connor's first
edition of *Orthodoxy* with 'When throwing a waste-paper
basket over the head of a clear-minded and virtuous pontiff, it
is unnecessary to inscribe many explanatory words upon
porcelain.'[15] No doubt Father O'Connor fathomed its meaning.

Charles Gatty had never seen George Wyndham laugh so
much as when he read extracts to him from *The Wallet of Kai
Lung*, which was probably later that same August as Gatty and
Father O'Connor travelled straight from Beach House to the
Wyndhams' home, Saighton Grange, part of the Grosvenor
estate near Chester. Father O'Connor later recalled[16] that the
old house glowed red and the colourful garden provided a
welcome sight after the bleached East Coast and the blackened
London and North Western Railway by which they had
travelled. They met their host striding across the lawns, a
tennis racquet in his hand, looking for his guests. During the
following days, while Charles was undergoing an operation for
the removal of a carbuncle, the priest was once more treated to
good company and good conservation with long discussions on
poetry and literature with George. He thought that if George's
conversations were printed they would look better than most
leading articles in newspapers as he never spoke an idle or
useless word.

Gradually Father O' Connor was working his way back to

Yorkshire. Robert Hudson wrote to him expressing how he had enjoyed his visit and insisting he must come again, as often as possible, either to Beach House or to his London home, in Dean's Yard, Westminster. Robert's mother was a little disturbed at first by her son's intimate friendship with a papist, but the priest quickly became her friend, even after he had opened all doors for Robert and his daughter when they had visited Rome. They presented him with a rosary which had been blessed by the Pope but in spite of a very enjoyable visit they remained staunch Anglicans.

After the summer holidays it was back to school for Father O'Connor, Dr Hinsley and the boys of St Bede's. Writing in a *Souvenir of St Bede's Grammar School,* published when the new school was opened in 1939, an old boy remembered being deprived of Father O'Connor's 'brilliant and deep learning' after only a short time as the priest was once again given a new posting. Much to his distress, Father O'Connor found himself appointed curate at the Church of the Holy Family in New Wortley, Leeds. He was not at all happy with the move and complained of being sad and lonely and much too unsettled to do anything as he had been told he was only there until something else came along. He was very sick at heart, more so than for a long time, and was just waiting for better things while the constant changes had begun to weary him as he already had so many books and objects to trail round with him. What he most disliked was the town itself which reminded him of the east end of London. Pouring all this out in a letter to Gatty[17] had helped him, he just hoped it hadn't done any harm to the recipient still recovering from his indisposition at Saighton.

Father O'Connor continued to complain to Gatty[18] that he felt very abused and through no fault of his own, he also felt a bit mean for burdening his friend again with his troubles. The priest now hoped for a quiet country place as he had had enough of towns. Being overworked at Halifax and other problems there had been touched on in earlier letters when he told Gatty that the excellent housekeeper at St Marie's was unable to stand it there any longer and was leaving.[19] This was about the time he, himself, was waiting for the governors of St Bede's to sort out his accommodation. There were obviously more problems in Halifax and Bradford than were referred to in print but Father O'Connor felt he was richer for the experience and that he had been rewarded by great graces for simply carrying out his sacerdotal work.

Early in November Father O'Connor had been told by a friend in the Council of Bishops that a vacancy in the country was now only weeks away. The post would most likely be a chaplaincy with a good house and one hundred and twenty pounds a year. He was already planning for Charles Gatty to visit him regularly, and suggested it might be more convenient to leave a nightshirt and toothbrush with Father O'Connor permanently in case of an unplanned visit to him. The situation never materialized, and the end of 1901 saw Father O'Connor still at New Wortley, and chaplain at Armley Gaol, where the Catholics were turning to the Church of England. He asked Gatty to pray for a nice place for him as was sick of being a curate when what he really wanted was to paddle his own canoe.[20]

Virtually all the letters between Gatty and Father O'Connor at this time contain discussions of the hymns the latter was writing or translating for the hymnal, indeed this is the reason they have survived. Tucked in with other correspondence regarding the hymnal I was surprised and delighted when I came upon them. Father O'Connor's prayers were not answered in the way he had hoped and his next move, in 1902, was again as a curate, in this instance to Canon Watson at St Anne's in Keighley, near Bradford. God had no intention of letting the little Irish man vegetate in a quiet country parish. He had much bigger plans for him, plans that would bring him to the notice of the whole world, bringing him fame if not fortune.

Notes

1. Brown, 'A Layman's Tribute', *Yorkshire Catholic Monthly*.
2. O'Connor, *Father Brown's Mixed Memories*.
3. O'Connor, *Father Brown on Chesterton*, p. 16.
4. O'Connor, *Father Brown's Mixed Memories*.
5. O'Connor, *Annals of the Poor*.
6. O'Connor, *Letter*, 13 December 1898, Downside Abbey.
7. O'Connor, *Letter*, 6 February 1899, ibid.
8. O'Connor, *Letter*, 2 March 1901, ibid.
9. Ibid.
10. O'Connor, *Letter*, Passion Tide 1901, ibid.
11. Wyndham, *Letters of George Wyndham*, 8 August 1901.
12. Spender, *Sir Robert Hudson*, pp. 81–2.
13. Ibid., p. 83.
14. O'Connor, *Father Brown on Chesterton*, p. 104.
15. Ibid., p. 103.
16. Gatty, *George Wyndham Recognita*.
17. O'Connor, *Letter*, 1901. Downside Abbey.
18. O'Connor, *Letter,* 8 October 1901, ibid.
19. O'Connor, *Letter*, 2 March 1901, ibid.
20. O'Connor, *Letter*, 8 November 1901, ibid.

Chapter 3

1902–05: G. K. Chesterton meets a Catholic Curate

St Anne's church, Keighley, designed by Augustus Welby Pugin, was opened in November 1840 but by the time Father O'Connor arrived in 1902 it had become inadequate for the needs of the large congregation. Four Sunday services were needed because of lack of space but by 1903, two of them were able to be held at the same time, one in the church and one in the new school. The St Anne's Catholic Association catered for all interests, both intellectual and physical, but in spite of the many activities taking place within the parish community causing the Canon and his two curates a heavy workload, Father O'Connor managed to not only maintain his own wide social circle but actually to extend it.

In October 1902, Father O'Connor, received part five of the *Arundel Hymns*, and thought that it was the best part yet. The correspondence in the archive ends here, but of course Father O'Connor's friendship with Charles Gatty continued. The following February saw the start of the long correspondence and, subsequently, the long and intimate friendship with Gilbert Keith and Frances Chesterton for which Father O'Connor is most widely known.

The first letter in the G. K. Chesterton Papers[1] dates from 11 February 1903, when Father O'Connor introduced himself to Chesterton as a Catholic priest who thanked God for having given Chesterton the spirituality which alone made literature immortal. This observation was based on his reading of *The*

Defendant, Chesterton's recently published first book of collected essays, and *Twelve Types*, his second. The phrase the 'foolish and valiant heart of man' in *The Defendant*, gave him great pleasure each time he thought of it, while of particular appeal in *Twelve Types*, were the essays on St Francis, Savonarola and Walter Scott. The priest managed to squeeze in references in the first sentence to *Buck Fanshaw 's Funeral*, the Mark Twain short story, and Oliver Wendell Holmes's *The Autocrat of the Breakfast Table*, for which Chesterton wrote a preface when it was published in England the following year. Father O'Connor thus managed to establish not only his literary credentials with regard to English and American literature, but also recognized Chesterton's spiritual leanings in the first half dozen lines of the letter. There would be no shortage of subjects to discuss when the two met.

The letter elicited a response from Chesterton for which Father O'Connor could only have wished. G. K.'s reply included the hope that he would be able to visit the priest when he was in Keighley, in December, to lecture to the Literary Society. Father O'Connor was, of course, delighted and offered Chesterton a bed for the night. He was slightly worried he might have to brush-up on the Brontës in order to converse with Chesterton as personally he found them tiresome, however he was prepared to do it for the sake of friendship. With Haworth, the home of the Brontë sisters, being on Keighley's doorstep, the Brontës tended to be a topic every visitor wished to discuss.

Frances Chesterton then took up the correspondence on behalf of her husband who was too busy to do so himself. Gilbert had promised to stay with Herbert Hugill, a prominent local figure and secretary of the Keighley Literary and Scientific Society, but he still wanted to meet the priest, who was relieved to hear that Chesterton would rather discuss the 'valiant and foolish heart of man' or St Francis rather than the Brontës. After this the long correspondence was mainly carried on by Frances and through it developed a friendship that was as close, if not more so, than that which the priest had with her husband.

There is a question mark over the date when Father O'Connor and Chesterton, famous at this time as a London journalist, had their first meeting which was followed next day by the walk together that would have such unforeseen consequences. Though the meeting and the walk are well documented in various books, the facts are unreliable. Unfortunately, we can't rely on even the

IN MEMORY OF
HERBERT HUGILL M.B.E.
BORN JULY 27TH 1872
DIED FEBRUARY 21ST 1919.
SEC. OF THE KEIGHLEY WAR
SAVINGS ASSOCIATION AND
SEC. FOR 10 YEARS OF THE
KEIGHLEY LITERARY SOCIETY.

"Death opens unknown
doors: it is most
grand to die"

Herbert Hugill memorial. G. K. Chesterton met Fr O'Connor at Hugill's house.

principals' own accounts. In his autobiography,[2] Chesterton recalled this walk, taken after he had given a lecture in Keighley. He remembered staying overnight with a leading citizen and the following morning setting off with his new friend, the priest, to visit his old friends, the Steinthal family. As to what date this took place, the only clue he gives is that it was during the early days, around the time of his marriage, in 1901.

In *Father Brown on Chesterton,*[3] Father O'Connor is more specific, stating that the two of them met at Herbert Hugill's house at Keighley in the spring of 1904. They agreed to walk together, on the following day, over the moors to Ilkley where Chesterton was to spend a short holiday with friends. The March wind was blowing as they strode across the fine Yorkshire moorland where Father O'Connor achieved his heart's desire of conversation with Chesterton. They discussed GK's lecture of the previous evening entitled *Modern Thought* and, reflecting on this idea of everyone wanting everything both ways, Father O'Connor regaled him with tales of the Bradford Workhouse. During the course of this long walk, they covered many subjects which included Zola, Confession, and Maria Monk's bitterly anti-clerical account of life in a

Keighley Moor where G. K. Chesterton and Fr O'Connor took the famous walk, and 'Fr Brown' was born.

Canadian convent which had recently appeared on local book stalls. Maria Monk subsequently found her way into a Chesterton essay. It took four chapters for Father O'Connor to record their walk before they reached their destination, where they were greeted by Mrs Chesterton and all sat down to shepherd's pie. All straightforward it seems, except, from the evidence, it couldn't have happened like this at all!

The first meeting of the illustrious pair took place on Thursday, 3 December 1903, when Chesterton delivered a lecture, entitled *The Shyness of the Journalist,* to the Keighley Literary and Scientific Society. Herbert Hugill, who had revived the Scientific Society and developed its literary side, presided. A full account of the lecture appeared the following Saturday in the weekly *Keighley News.* I have found no evidence of *Modern Thought*, the lecture which Father O'Connor 'remembered' so well, nor have the Chesterton experts I have consulted any knowledge of it, so this remains a mystery. That Father O'Connor was at the Keighley meeting is verified by his letter to Mrs Chesterton on 6 December 1903,[4] in which he expressed his delight with the time he spent with 'the great big boy' at the lecture and the following day, Friday 4 December, when they walked together over the moors to Ilkley. There were no March winds on this hike, but they had been favoured by two hours of sunshine. Journey's end was the Steinthal family home, St John's, on the very edge of the moor, where Father O'Connor had enjoyed himself so much that eight hours had flown by as one. Frances Chesterton was obviously not there to greet them, but I don't dispute the shepherd's pie.

In a letter to Frances dated 6 December 1904,[5] Father O'Connor recalled that the previous Friday had been the anniversary of his introduction to St John's, further verification that he had been there in 1903. At the beginning of 1904, he told Frances that he was looking forward to seeing both herself and Gilbert at Ilkley at Easter. An entry made by Frances in her diary dated 5 April, Easter Tuesday,[6] records that Father O'Connor had come over and what, presumably, were her first impressions of him. She had found him to be delightful, both boyish and wise, young and old, with a charm she found difficult to define and though he used his hands to help express meaning it was never affected or theatrical. She thought it wonderful that 'he should lead the quiet life of a parish priest in Keighley when he appears so dazzling'. Of course he wasn't even a parish priest!

As the Chestertons were in Ilkley by 31 March and Frances didn't make daily diary entries, Father O'Connor may have been there at any time during the holiday, either for the day or have stayed over. The *Yorkshire Daily Observer*, for Tuesday 5 April, reported that the Easter weather at Ilkley had been wet and windy until the Monday when it was fine and breezy, in fact a bright, blustery day exactly as described by Father O'Connor in his book. Easter Monday was, and still is, a very popular day for walking over the moors between Bradford, Keighley and Ilkley, so it seems likely that Father O'Connor confused a walk taken during this holiday with the one that had taken place at the end of 1903, especially as the book was written over thirty years after the events he described in its opening pages, and after Chesterton's death. But there had been no lecture the night before at Keighley or anywhere else this time. Is it possible that the mystery lecture was in fact only a discussion on Modern Thought between Chesterton and the guests at St John's?

As the Steinthals played a large part in Father O'Connor's social life, and where the Chestertons were often to be found, now is a good time to discover a little more about this interesting family. Francis Frederick Steinthal was the head of the family and of the yarn export firm established in Bradford by his father Charles Gustavus Steinthal of Frankfurt. He was on the council of the Bradford Chamber of Commerce and chairman of the Yarn Merchants section but he was also a philanthropist and sometime chairman of the Bradford Charity Organization Society. He impressed Father O'Connor with his immense charm and integrity.

Mrs Steinthal, Emmeline, was the daughter of a Lancashire Justice of the Peace. During the First World War, her three sons thought it expedient to change their name and took her

family name of Petrie. Their sister, Dorothea, was bolder, or
foolish, and kept her German name even when a nurse in a
frontline hospital. Emmeline trained as a painter and sculptor,
first at Manchester and then in Paris, and exhibited several
times at the Royal Academy. Both she and her husband were
founding members of the Ilkley Guild of Help, and continued
to work hard on their behalf. At a time when there was no
National Health scheme, unemployment benefit or pension
provision, the Guild sought to help less fortunate residents
through all kinds of difficulties, not merely financial ones.

Emmeline was an active member of many worthwhile
organizations, too numerous to mention here, but she took a
great interest in education. Having read *Home Education* and
discovering that its author, Charlotte Mason, lived in Bradford,
Emmeline visited her to discuss the education of her four
children. Later she invited several friends to meet Charlotte,
who had drawn up an outline plan of both a method of home
education and a training of teachers. This led to the formation of
a Parents' Educational Union with the aim of studying education
as it impinged on the physical development, moral training,
intellectual life and moral upbringing of children. This in turn
led to the Parents' National Educational Union (PNEU) with
numerous branches and a headquarters in London. The Union
secretary was one Frances Blogg, who resigned her post in 1900
to spend a few months abroad before marrying a certain Mr
Gilbert Chesterton, after which she introduced him to her friends
the Steinthals.

The Steinthal house was dedicated to the 'Beloved Disciple',
and an enamel of St John's emblem was over the hearth in the
middle room of the house. The house was designed by Norman
Shaw with interior design by John Aldam Heaton, for the
latter's brother-in-law, John William Atkinson. Heaton was a
Bradford man who gave William Morris one of his first
commissions, and had Rossetti to stay in his house while he
designed stained glass for the windows, thus starting a trend for
Morris windows amongst the wealthy merchants of Bradford.
Heaton eventually moved to London to work full-time with
Shaw.

St John's Ilkley, the home of the Steinthal family, to where Chesterton and Fr O'Connor were walking.

In 1885, the house was auctioned and the notice in the *Ilkley Gazette* stressed how every care had been taken to ensure comfort, the efficient and costly heating of all the reception rooms, hall and landings, and the excellent sanitary arrangements. The lounge, dining room and drawing room were apartments of noble proportions. The garden, through which a stream wound, boasted fine trees and shrubs. Magnificent views over some of the loveliest scenery in Wharfedale were to be had from both house and garden. When the Steinthals moved into the house in 1900, they employed ten maids to look after it and the family but Emmeline treated them all as friends and taught them many skills. St John's was converted into flats in the 1950s and has recently been fully refurbished into nine modern apartments but the stone fireplace with its inscribed lintel has been preserved. The magnificent building, albeit with a rather ugly modern extension, was honoured in January 2008 with a heritage blue plaque awarded by the Ilkley Civic Society. The blue plaque also marks the author of the 'Father Brown' stories, G. K. Chesterton's association with the house. The newspaper report mentioned that Father Brown was based on a Catholic priest Chesterton met at Keighley but not that he too was a frequent visitor to the house they both loved.

I went to Burgess Hill to visit Christine Deegan, daughter of Telford Petrie, the eldest Steinthal son, who was very proud to be custodian of the Visitors' Book from her grandparents' house. Among the famous signatures, she showed me a sketch of an eagle and a song, entitled *St John's Legend*, both by Chesterton. I was also pleased to discover that the large wing chair in which I was sitting had been made especially for Gilbert, as her grandmother had feared for her spindly chairs when Gilbert's large bulk descended on them. Hilaire Belloc was occasionally at St John's at the same time as Gilbert Chesterton and she still had a poem written there by Chesterbelloc.

Mrs Deegan remembered the Chestertons visiting them when they lived in Manchester, but when they first knew them Gilbert and Frances were Uncle Blobs and Aunty Dibbs to her father and his siblings at St John's. Her last memory of Gilbert was when they were all in Brighton not long before he died. She described Frances being like a dainty little piece of china, very pretty in blue tweeds. She had a good sense of humour but had not been amused when a lady came up to Gilbert and asked for his autograph as they were sitting having tea in the Queen's Hotel. She was always very protective of him so was annoyed when this family occasion was interrupted when he walked off with her. He came back chuckling however, having taken a short time to write a long poem in the lady's book, all about people wanting autographs when other people were having tea! In May 1904, Father O'Connor and the Steinthals were at the Bradford Exhibition which took place to celebrate the opening of the Art Gallery and Museum in the newly built Cartwright Memorial Hall by the Prince and Princess of Wales. Francis Steinthal was a vice-president of the exhibition, while his wife was chairman of the Women's Section. Under the auspices of the latter, a series of conferences were held on some aspect of educational work. Walter Crane, the artist and book illustrator who was staying with the Steinthals, gave the first lecture entitled *Design*. Father O'Connor seconded the Dean of Durham's vote of thanks. Walter Crane and Father O'Connor discussed the Chestertons at length as the artist had read and enjoyed GK's recently published book on the painter and sculptor, G. F. Watts, and was now anxious to meet him.

The evening lecture had been given by Alfred Drury, whose statue of Queen Victoria in full regalia had been unveiled by the Prince of Wales on his recent visit to Bradford. The famous sculptor modelled a bust from life of the professional model he had brought from London. The seventy-year-old patriarchal-looking man had posed in so gorgeous a manner as to remind Father O'Connor of Dante stuck for a rhyme!

About this time, Father O'Connor had been amused to hear that Gilbert was starting to write detective stories. He had thought of suggesting what a good story could be made by GK 'about a guileless and earnest Bishop having to censure doctrinal differences which no one can identify'[7] but then he thought they would have little chance of publication. Chesterton's stories were published a year later in 1905 as *The Club of Queer Trades* with detectives Rupert and Basil Grant. Father Brown had yet to be born.

The Chestertons and Father O'Connor were together again at St John's on 23 August to celebrate the fiftieth birthday of Francis Steinthal. The main event at the celebration was the performance of a masque, entitled *Titania's Prophecy*, which had been especially written for the occasion by Gilbert, in which a fairy foresees a great house called St John's, occupied by a 'Steinthal' who would be King of the Kingdom of St John's.

Family photographs of the actors in the garden show the three Steinthal sons, Francis Eric, Telford and Paul, as King John, King Stephen and Robin Hood, with their sister, Dorothea, as Maid Marion. The script of the play features a King Henry instead of King John but this may have been changed at a later date or it may be an error as there are a number of mistakes in the introduction. The remaining two parts of the Spirit of England and the Fairy were taken by family friends Grace Raine and Rhoda Bastaple respectively.

A book of war songs, entitled *Songs of the Sword and the Soldier*, collected and edited by Alexander Eager, was reviewed by Chesterton in *The Speaker* in 1901.[8] It was some years later when Father O'Connor came across this review and when he read the lines 'the thing which is admired in the soldier is not the accomplishment of killing, but the more elegant accomplishment of being killed',[9] the priest was 'almost purring'.[10] He found that Chesterton had expressed in 1901, the same sentiments as he himself had preached at a soldier's funeral in 1898, that is 'that the glory of a soldier is not in going forth to kill but in his carrying his own life lightly in his hand'.[11]

In December Father O'Connor decided to part with a painting from his large art collection and sold it to the National Gallery in London for £200, although it would have been worth more, due to its rarity if it had also been offered in Paris. As he told Frances,[12] he preferred to have the picture in the National Gallery for two hundred pounds rather than nowhere in particular (could he mean Paris?) at twice the amount. Some very good detective work on the part of Alan Crookham, archivist at The National Gallery, discovered that the work in question is probably *The Virgin and Child*, a fifteenth-century painting by Lazzaro Bastiani. It is believed that Father O'Connor bought the painting at a local sale, then sold it to the National Art Collections Fund to donate to the National Gallery. It is currently in store but there is an image on the National Gallery website.

Father O'Connor was quite an authority on art and a great collector with an eye for the real thing. Herbert Hugill's sister, Annie, gave weekly art classes at St Anne's school, and, though Father O'Connor had never met her, he had seen some of her own work in local exhibitions. He considered her to be of the Impressionist School and thought that she would be heard more of as an artist. He was right in his prediction as, although she was a teacher all her life, her watercolours were exhibited from time to time at the Royal Academy. After her death she left the residue, after minor legacies, of a not insubstantial estate to the Royal Academy to set up a fund in order to buy pictures from their exhibitions to present to public art galleries.

Canon Watson died from cardiac asthma, aged only sixty-four, in March 1905 but it wasn't here that Father O'Connor was finally given the chance to paddle his own canoe. Instead, Father Russell was transferred from Heckmondwike to take over from the Canon, but Father O'Connor was, at last, given his own parish when he stepped into Father Russell's shoes at Heckmondwike.

Notes

1. O'Connor, *Letter*, 11 February 1903, 31–2, British Library.
2. Chesterton, *Autobiography*, pp. 324–5.
3. O'Connor, *Father Brown on Chesterton*, pp.1–27.
4. O'Connor, *Letter*, 6 December 1903, 37–8, British Library.
5. O'Connor, *Letter*, 6 December 1904, 55–6, ibid.
6. Mackey, 'Diary of Frances Chesterton', *The Chesterton Review*, p. 286.
7. O'Connor, *Letter*, 29 June 1904, 49–50, British Library.
8. Chesterton, 'A Book of War-Songs', *The Speaker*, pp. 255–6.
9. Chesterton,'A Book of War-Songs', *The Speaker*, p. 255.
10. O'Connor, *Letter*, 25 September 1904, 53–4, British Library.
11. Ibid.
12. O'Connor, *Letter*, 6 December 1904, 55–6, ibid.

Chapter 4

1905–19: Father O'Connor Builds his First Church

In the spring of 1905, Father O'Connor was so caught up in what he called 'the very harassing and engrossing occupation of flitting'[1] (moving home) to Heckmondwike, that it was some time before he was able to answer his latest missive from Frances Chesterton. Unfortunately we don't know what she wrote in that letter, but from the priest's reply it seems she was in need of a sympathetic ear which Gilbert was failing to provide. Father O'Connor thought that her husband was physically unable to stay still long enough, due to the intense workings of his brain, to provide passive sympathy or the power of listening which was the only real help we can give one another in trouble. He wisely pointed out that when we need to blow off steam advice might be good, but the only really soothing influence is the silence of the other party. God, being the most passive of all listeners, is the only perfect sympathizer.

Father O'Connor offered helpful advice on coping with the cross which Frances felt she carried and her distress in feeling that she was not carrying it well. The particular cross to which she referred may have been the very painful arthritis of the spine she suffered for many years. Few of even her intimate friends knew of this and she was not known for complaining but she held little back from Father O'Connor during their long friendship. However, another ongoing, grave concern was her brother, Knollys, who suffered recurring bouts of depression after the death of their sister Gertrude. Frances had already asked Father O'Connor to write to him encouraging Knollys when he could but not to be put off by any rebuffs and it seems likely that this is what was troubling her most.

It was late summer, just after he had returned from his annual visit to Robert Hudson at Felixstowe, that Father O'Connor replied[2] to another letter from Frances Chesterton which showed she was still very troubled. He wondered if the black despair Frances had mentioned was a mental or nervous malady; he thought it was probably the latter and, if so, was surely a passing cloud. He didn't know the priest she mentioned and wished he knew the right person to recommend. Again, from only the reply, it is not possible to tell who suffered from black despair but it does seem to have been Knollys. Some time later he appeared to have made a good recovery but on 25 August the following year, Frances broke the dreadful news that he had drowned himself in the sea at Seaford in Sussex. Her brother had recently converted to Catholicism and attended Mass in the morning before he taking his life the same evening. Whatever the nature of the cross she carried, it is a measure of the esteem in which Frances held her new friend, that she discussed matters so close to her heart barely a year after they first met.

Father O'Connor at last had his first parish, and what a remarkable change he wrought there during the fourteen years of his stay. The parish had started life in a rented room but, in 1872, land had been bought and a school built which also served as a chapel. Father Russell had introduced the idea of a separate church and had started a scheme to finance it, but it was left to Father O'Connor to continue fundraising and build the church.

One of the first things he did was to introduce his parishioners to Elgar in a concert featuring the *Dream of Gerontius* on three Sunday evenings. Father O'Connor was pleased with its reception by the audience of colliers and rag-pickers and considered the manner in which it was received to be infinitely better than that of an audience in the stalls of a London or Bradford theatre. He next wanted to start a dancing class for the children, some of whom were already adept at Irish reel, so Father O'Connor turned to Frances for advice on the essentials needed for the project.

Not only had his parishioners music and dancing, they also had the benefit of a travelling theatre, or 'Penny Gaff', which took over the village green for three months, performing the plays in a tent. Father O'Connor delighted in sending their playbills to Gilbert Chesterton who returned them with the titles altered so, for instance, *The Lady in Red, or the Power of a Mother's Love* became *The Lady in Bed, or the Power of Mrs Eddy's Love*. Similarly, *The Shaughran,* became *The Shaw Grin.* The village green was not so much a green as a cinder patch which was later laid out as a park to commemorate the coronation of King George V and Queen Mary.

Father O'Connor's first home in Heckmondwike was a rented property in St James Street and it wasn't until 1911 that 'Fieldhead' was acquired for £1,000. This provided an elevated prime site for the new church overlooking Heckmondwike; it was to become a notable landmark. The new parish priest immediately moved in and started a fundraising campaign, making personal appeals throughout the diocese which, together with private subscriptions, raised £500.

Not one to shirk his duty to his parish, Father O'Connor's personal contribution was to auction his art collection. His Continental education, especially the years spent in Rome, had brought him a knowledge and love of art which, together with his natural instinct for the genuine article, had enabled him to amass a quite remarkable collection over the past fifteen years. He became well known for this ability and Edward Macdonald, an associate of Chesterton's on *G. K's Weekly*, recalled an instance when they were both discussing pictures in the refectory of a religious establishment, Father O'Connor insisted that a highly prized painting was in fact an inferior copy, while another lightly regarded one was an original of much greater value. His opinion carried so much weight that the pictures were re-examined and he was indeed proved to be right.

The collection was auctioned at the British Galleries in Bradford on 12 June 1913. That day the bidders went home with many a bargain as the amount raised, around £1,000, was not as much as might have been expected, although the auctioneers regarded it as the finest collection, due to exceptionally good judgement and taste, to have gone under the hammer for some considerable time. However, two pictures, both by J. W. Buxton Knight, reached three figures: *Rain Passing Over* drew the most competition and was sold for 150gns. while *Path through the Fir Woods* raised 120gns. Replying to comments on the great sacrifice he had made, Father O'Connor replied that he if he had lost one thing he had gained another; he now had a church instead of the pictures. But he was soon rummaging around the salerooms of the West Riding again and gradually amassed another valuable art collection.

The fundraising continued throughout the summer with garden parties at Fieldhead, one with 200 people raised ten pounds and another with 100 raised six pounds. Collections were made among both past and present parishioners, ten pounds came from parishioners who had emigrated to America. Of course the priest's own friends supported the cause: Frances Chesterton, who had been staying with George Wyndham and his wife, passed on all Lady Grosvenor's kind wishes but said she had characteristically forgotten to give her the promised pound to send on. This throws into perspective the value of a pound at the time and the real worth of the amount raised by Father O'Connor himself.

Pentecost, or Whit Sunday, commemorates the descent of the Holy Spirit upon the Apostles, so this was an appropriate day to erect the plain wooden cross on the site of the high altar of the new Church of the Holy Spirit. The following day, 1 June 1914, the Right Revd Dr Cowgill, Lord Bishop of Leeds, laid the foundation stone. Crowds lined the streets as the procession, led by the Cleckheaton Temperance band and the Boys' Brigade from Our Lady and St Paulinus' church, Dewsbury with their bugles and drums, made their way from the school to the site. It was a colourful procession with a large contingent of robed clergy; the Bishop himself wore his cope and mitre and little girls, dressed in white, carried garlands or baskets of flowers while others marched with banners.

Just fifteen months later, on 29 September 1915, the Bishop was back in Heckmondwike to celebrate the first Mass in the new church. Father O'Connor was responsible for the Byzantine-Romanesque design, its blend of eastern and western elements reminiscent of the old Mediterranean Christian churches brought a new dimension to the architecture of the area. The octagonal dome was supported by four arches on top of granite columns which had been brought by sea from Norway during the early days of the First World War, escorted by the Royal Navy.

The Revd H. E. G. Rope's sister, Margaret Agnes Rope (Marga), a reputable stained glass artist, designed the east window of the new church. This comprised three round windows, the centre one, over the altar, depicting a descending dove, symbol of the Holy Spirit, with St John, now damaged, and St George on either side. Her brother had stayed with Father O'Connor in 1912 and they had visited local missions together, praying the rosary as they went. Perhaps the idea for the east window was mooted at the same time. The altar was only temporary and when the new one was consecrated in 1933 Father O'Connor returned from St Cuthbert's to sing the Solemn High Mass. The church would accommodate 260 people and had cost an estimated £2,500.

1911 saw the publication of Chesterton's great epic poem *The Ballad of the White Horse*, in which the author incorporates popular legends in the fictitious tale of King Alfred's battles with the Danes, culminating in his victory at Ethandune. The White Horse of the title refers to that which is carved out of a hillside in Berkshire, only some thirty miles away from Beaconsfield to where the Chestertons had moved a couple of years previously. Frances Chesterton told Father O'Connor of the epic being contemplated by her husband, which he saw immediately, as she gave him a few sample lines, was greatly loved by her. He hoped his own delight in the examples was a help to its composition.

The poem was some time in the making, so Father O'Connor had a number of opportunities to put forward his own thoughts and ideas. He remembered remarking one day when they were

The Church of the Holy Spirit, Heckwondwike: the east window. The first church built by Fr O'Connor; the east window was designed by his friend, Fr H. E. G. Rope's sister.

all at St John's how even great men relied on lesser ones, the servants, getting up first, lighting fires and preparing breakfast before they themselves could start their own day. This resulted in Chesterton writing a passage, between the dressing-bell and dinner, elaborating this idea and beginning: 'And well may God with the serving folk Cast in His dreadful lot; Is not He too a servant, And is not He forgot?'[3] These lines appear in Book IV, *The Woman in the Forest,* but the priest considered the previous section, entitled *The Harp of Alfred,* contained some of the best lyric thinking in all the literature he knew. Unfortunately, he didn't think any of his suggestions had contributed to the immortal lines it contained. Father O'Connor felt that he had suggested or inspired so much more of this work than he ever did to *Father Brown,* and was thrilled when Frances presented him with the whole manuscript to censor as so much of his was in it. When Father O'Connor received his copy of *The Ballad of the White Horse,* he asked the Gilbert to inscribe it. The following was the result:

To Father O'Connor – G. K. Chesterton[4]

The scratching pen, the aching tooth,
The Plea for Higher Unity,
The aged buck, the earnest youth,
The Missing Link, the Busy Bee,
The Superman, the Third Degree
Are things that I should greatly like
To take and sling quite suddenly
As far as Heaven from Heckmondwike.

As far as Hood is from Fitzooth,
As far as seraphs from a flea,
As far as Campbell from the truth,
Or old Bohemia from the sea,
Or Shakespeare from Sir Herbert Tree
Or Nathan from an Arab sheik,
Or most of us from £. s. d.
As far as Heaven from Heckmondwike.

As far as actresses from youth,
As far, as far as lunch from tea,
As far as Horton from Maynooth,
As far as Paris from Paree;
As far as Hawke is from a gee,

Or I am from an old high bike,
As far as Stead from sanity,
As far as Heaven from Heckmondwike.

Envoi
Prince, Cardinal, that is to be,
Cardinals do not go on strike
I'm far from wishing it (D.V.)
As far as Heaven from Heckmondwike.

A number of intended visits by Frances and Gilbert were thwarted by bad weather, illness or sheer lack of time in Yorkshire, but Gilbert did lunch with Father O'Connor at Fieldhead in May 1911. It is possible that he brought a copy of his new book for his friend on that day and that he wrote the poem while he was there.

GK had been rather more complimentary to Heckmondwike in a poem inscribed in Father O'Connor's bright-orange jacketed copy of *The Ball and the Cross*, published a couple of years earlier in 1909, which Father O'Connor took with him to Beaconsfield to be inscribed.

This is a book I do not like,[5]
Take it away to Heckmondwike,
A lurid exile, lost and sad
To punish it for being bad.
You need not take it from the shelf
(I tried to read it once myself:
The speeches jerk, the chapters sprawl,
The story makes no sense at all)
Hide it your Yorkshire moors among
Where no man speaks the English tongue.

Hail Heckmondwike! Successful spot!
Saved from the Latin's festering lot,
Where Horton and where Hocking see,
The grace of Heaven, Prosperity.

Above the chimneys, hung and bowed
A pillar of most solid cloud;

To starved oppressed Italian eyes,
The place would seem a Paradise,
And many a man from Como Lake,
And many a Tyrolese would take
(If priests allowed them what they like)
Their holidays in Heckmondwike.

The Belgian with his bankrupt woes,
Who through deserted Brussels goes,
The hind that threads those ruins bare,
Where Munich and Milan were –
Hears owls and wolves howl like Gehenna
In the best quarters of Vienna,
Murmurs in tears, 'Ah, how unlike
The happiness of Heckmondwike!'

In Spain the sad guitar they strike,
And, yearning, sing of Heckmondwike;
The Papal Guard leans on his pike
And dreams he is in Heckmondwike.
Peru's proud horsemen long to bike
But for one hour in Heckmondwike;
Offered a Land Bill, Pat and Mike
Cry: 'Give us stones! – in Heckmondwike!'
Bavarian Bier is good, belike:
But try the gin of Heckmondwike.
The Flamands drown in ditch and dyke
Their itch to be in Heckmondwike:
Rise, Freedom, with the sword to strike!
And turn the world to Heckmondwike.

Take then this book I do not like –
It may improve in Heckmondwike.

Father O'Connor and the Chestertons spent so much time in each other's company that ideas rubbed off on Gilbert, or were the result of discussions, more often than may be suspected. After they had taken part in a discussion at the Ladies' Debating Society at Leeds, led by Gilbert, that all wars were religious wars, the priest told him about the Battle of Lepanto.

This sixteenth-century naval engagement between the fleets of the Ottoman Empire and the Holy League was led by Don John of Austria and resulted in victory for the Christians. This led to the appearance some years later, on the anniversary of the battle, 7 October, of Chesterton's *Ballad of Lepanto*. Or so Father O'Connor believed.

There was always room for discussion at the dinner table at St John's and Home Rule for Ireland was the topic on one occasion. Mr and Mrs Steinthal were in favour, as was Chesterton, so when he was asked by his host what case could be made for Home Rule, Father O'Connor launched into a monologue that was duly noted by Gilbert. When *Crimes of England* was published in 1915, Father O'Connor recognized some of the things he had spoken about, although his family relationships had been slightly manipulated so that now he had a brother and his grandmother had become his mother.

In 1913, while his new church was still at the planning stage, Father O'Connor was invited to preach the *Weld Sermon*. Monsignor Weld had studied at Downside, Douai and Rome before reaching high office at the papal court, but he preferred to be an ordinary priest in England. In his old age he asked that he be allowed to go and preach everywhere on the love and goodness of God. To enable the work to continue after his death, he endowed an annual sermon to be preached on 'The Love and Goodness of God', the preacher to be chosen by the Abbot of Downside. After the event, the Abbot had to ensure its printing and distribution. Father O'Connor preached the sermon at St Benedict's church in Hindley, now part of Greater Manchester, taking as his theme, 'God's Love for Man as Manifested in and Through His Church'.

Chesterton's play, *Magic,* was first performed in London in November 1913 and Frances was anxious that Father O'Connor should see it. More than once she urged him to make the trip, saying she would put him in the wings if only he would come. The new church and parish duties appear to have left him little spare time as he never did manage to see it, but Frances promised that, should it make a profit, some of it would find its way to Heckmondwike.

In a somewhat intriguing letter written in March 1914,[6] Frances enclosed three pounds ten shillings and asked Father O'Connor to send the weapons, which sounded 'glorious'. Gilbert said they would come in useful when the Social Revolution came. They arrived at Beaconsfield the following month and were hung on a fitting specially made for them in the studio, where, as far as we know, they remained, never a shot being fired from them, even if that were possible. They were probably antique weapons which Father O'Connor had discovered during his wanderings in the odd places where he discovered the occasional valuable painting.

Frances regretted that they had not managed to meet each other when Father O'Connor had been in London recently, but she was not surprised as she knew Father O'Connor was busy with meetings with his Australian aborigines.[7] It is more likely that his meeting was with one of the Benedictine monks of New Norcia, a mission started in Western Australia by Spanish Benedictines after their monasteries in Spain had been closed by the Government in 1835. Their founder, Bishop Rosendo Salvado, who had died in 1900, had visited Douai when the young John O'Connor was a student, and had regaled them with tales of teaching his naked aborigines how to play cricket! The monks did rather more for the indigenous children than teach them to play cricket of course, providing them with care and education. Father O'Connor may have met the Bishop again when the latter was on one of his fundraising visits to England, and with his love of children and their education, have become a supporter of their work.

Apart from contributing the odd book review to the *New Witness,* which was being edited by GK whilst his brother Cecil Chesterton was away helping win the war, Father O'Connor's last major work while at Heckmondwike appeared in 1918. This was a commentary on Francis Thompson's poem *The Mistress of Vision,* with a preface by Father Vincent McNabb, and published by Douglas Pepler at Ditchling. Father McNabb praised Father O'Connor's commentary, calling him 'the maker of many translations and therefore the lock-smith of many subtle thoughts'[8] who had 'turned his craft on one of the most subtle works of the century'.[9] The outward appearance of the book matched the quality of the writing, not only was the printing magnificent, but it was on thin handmade paper, the remaining batch of a stock made originally for William Morris and bought up by Pepler.

The following year, 1919, Father O' Connor made his final move to Bradford and the parish of St Cuthbert's, where he remained until his death some thirty years later but this in no way clipped his wings.

Notes

1. O'Connor, *Letter*, 17 May 1905, 57-8, British Library.
2. O'Connor, *Letter*, 18 September 1905, 59-60, ibid.
3. O'Connor, *Father Brown on Chesterton*, p. 63.
4. Ibid., p.109.
5. Ibid., p.110.
6. Chesterton, F. *Letter*, 13 March 1914, 95, British Library.
7. Chesterton, F. *Letter*, 30 April 1914, 100, ibid.
8. Thompson, *The Mistress of Vision*, Preface.
9. Ibid.

Chapter 5

Father Brown

Father Brown was 'born' on Ilkley Moor when both creator and original were once again visiting the Steinthal family. When exactly is a matter for speculation, as we have seen that neither Chesterton's nor Father O'Connor's memories for dates, recalled long after the event, tended to be accurate. According to Gilbert,[1] on this particular occasion Father O'Connor had attempted to correct Gilbert of a misconception with regard to questions of vice and crime by relating details of various perverted practices of which he was aware. This seems to accord with the account which Father O'Connor gave of the walk taken in 1904, discussed in Chapter 3, in which his tales of the workhouse, prison and the like were told. In a BBC radio broadcast, entitled *Father Brown*,[2] Father O'Connor mentions that the first stage of his development as Father Brown began on a walk on Ilkley moor during which the March winds were blowing, again indicating Easter 1904. When they reached the house, Father O'Connor discussed a variety of subjects, including music, architecture, and philosophy with a couple of Cambridge undergraduates who were very impressed by his knowledge. However, after he had left the room, one young man remarked that it was a shame the religious lived in such a cloistered environment, knowing nothing of the real evils of the world. It was the colossal irony of the remark that gave Chesterton, still shocked by his friend's revelations on the moor, the idea of a priest-detective, who knew more about the criminal mind than the criminals themselves. The students thought it was 'a very beautiful thing to be innocent and ignorant'[3] so it was perhaps fitting that the first collection of Father Brown stories was entitled *The Innocence of Father Brown*.

To further accentuate the contrast, which was the point of the comedy, Father O'Connor's character and appearance required a few changes. Chesterton turned 'his intelligent countenance into a condition of pudding-faced fatuity'.[4] The 'sensitive and quick-witted Irishman'[5] became 'a Suffolk dumpling from East Anglia'.[6] Father O'Connor 'was not shabby, but rather neat',[7] he was 'delicate and dexterous'[8] rather than 'clumsy',[9] and looked 'amusing and amused'.[10]

In a BBC radio broadcast in November 1936, Father O'Connor remarked how uncanny it was that Chesterton's fictional creation corresponded so well with his own, very reluctant, criticism of himself. The truth was that he was rather thick-set and pie-faced, if not pudding-faced, and rather pink. In fact he refrained from looking in the mirror as, if he did catch a glimpse of himself, he was saddened to discover he was not the tall, slender, pale intellectual with the regular clean-cut features of a filmstar that he was in his soul. Though he had never heard anyone admit to it, he suspected he was not the only person to have such a conflict between body and soul! He lamented that if only Chesterton had made him the way he wanted to be and never was! But that, of course, would have demolished the whole point of the stories. He liked the fact, however, that Chesterton had at least given him 'a tall sort of intellect and an incisive habit of looking at things'.[11]

Father O'Connor and his fictional counterpart did have some things in common. Father O'Connor had bought the flat hat he shared with Father Brown in Leeds but soon realized this had been a bad mistake, it being totally unsuitable for a small person, and it was soon discarded. Father O'Connor also had a large, cheap umbrella, which he preferred to an overcoat, and he too carried brown paper parcels 'having no sense of style in deportment'.[12]

Surprisingly, it was some time before Father O'Connor even

began to suspect that he might have been turned into a fictional detective, indeed he had read the first two collections of stories, published in 1911 and 1914, before so doing. Of course during those years he was rather preoccupied with art and church architecture. Even when he saw his portrait on the dust jacket of *The Innocence of Father Brown* he wasn't convinced until he later recollected some strange behaviour about a year earlier at the Steinthal dinner table. Sitting opposite him was Maria Zimmern, who had been scribbling away below the table, sitting next to her was Dorothea Steinthal who constantly looked first at himself and then at the drawing which occupied Maria and which subsequently appeared on the book cover. Maria Zimmern was a German artist and sculptor who exhibited in London and later married Eric Petrie (Steinthal). In 1927 she exhibited a bronze bust of Chesterton at the Spring Exhibition at Cartwright Hall, Bradford. Any suspicions Father O'Connor held on to were finally dispersed when he was introduced, by GK himself, to the company at Beaconsfield one evening as 'Father Brown'.

Father O'Connor thought Father Brown stemmed from the fact that he always noted small things, his ability of always being able to find the ashtray was considered miraculous by Chesterton who could never remember the time of day, nor yet what day it was. GK's memory was filled with recollections of everything he had ever heard or read, a feat which the priest found miraculous. When the detective stories were first conceived Frances Chesterton warned Father O'Connor not to let her husband pick his brains. The latter was more than welcome to any brains he had, but Father O'Connor felt that he had contributed more to Chesterton's more serious works and it was only in the first collection that Father O'Connor recognized anything he may have told his friend.

Father Brown was first introduced to the public in *The Blue Cross* in which the priest talks loudly about the silver cross set with blue stones that he is carrying. The idea of the blue stones themselves may have been suggested when Father O'Connor, with his usual eye for a bargain, had boasted to Chesterton that he had acquired five sapphires for five shillings, one of them being a particularly rich deep blue. What he did with these is not recorded, but they didn't lead to such an adventure as befell Father Brown.

The incident with the undergraduates at Ilkley creeps in at the end of both *The Blue Cross* and *The Flying Stars.* In the former, Father Brown replies to arch criminal Flambeau's question as to how he comes to know these criminal tricks, 'has it never struck you that a man who does next to nothing but hear men's real sins is not likely to be wholly unaware of human evil?'[13] At the end of the latter story, Sir Leopold tells the priest that 'though he himself had broader views, he could respect those whose creed required them to be cloistered and ignorant of this world'.[14]

Father O'Connor was well known for his wisdom, as was demonstrated by John Rothenstein where he likened Father O'Connor to a plumber, bringing forth words of wisdom, as and when necessary, as a plumber would bring out his tools. Both the priest's scholarly equipment and the plumber's tools would then be packed away until required further, so the title of the second collection of stories, *The Wisdom of Father Brown,* was again appropriate. It is possible to catch further glimpses of the non-fictional priest in the collections as he slips in and out of the tales, elusive as in his real life.

In *The Perishing of the Pendragons*, Father Brown and friends are visiting the home of Admiral Pendragon on the very night that another family member is due to die because of a curse on the property which seems to centre on a tower in the grounds. Father Brown asks the admiral if he may spend the night there, remarking 'Do you know that in my business you're an exorcist almost before anything else?'[15] This was true as Father O'Connor had become an exorcist, a minor order on the way to ordination, when he was at the English College so it was a subject he was familiar with and of which Chesterton was aware. Father Brown's activities at the Pendragon home, however, result in the capture of a criminal gang and exposure of a dastardly plot that has nothing at all to do with the supernatural. The detective's suspicions are first aroused by a chart of the river which everyone supposes to be a chart of Pacific islands, but he had recognized it by rocks shaped like a dragon and like Merlin.

'You seem to have noticed a lot when we came in', cried Fanshaw. 'We thought you were rather abstracted.'[16]

In *The Heaton Review* of 1934, Chesterton wrote 'A Note on Father Brown'. In the article he recalled that, while chatting one night with Father O'Connor, he asked a passing domestic for a box of matches. His friend drew his attention to a remote corner of the large room where a dim and distant shelf housed a number of insignificant dusty objects, among them a box of matches. 'It was a small thing but it did illustrate a habit of noticing a number of quite unnoticeable small things',[17] commented GK. The incident made a big enough impression on the author for him to sit down and compose a Father Brown crime story in which one man murders another with a box of matches. This duly appeared as *The Crime of the Communist* [18] but this propensity for observation of details had already been put to good use in the Pendragon story.

This incident with the matches was also recalled by Father O'Connor in *Father Brown on Chesterton* and took place in the lounge at Beaconsfield where a side table housed Gilbert's cigars and his matches, when he hadn't put them somewhere they could never be found. On this particular occasion, Father O'Connor had noticed that their only box of matches was behind a vase on a very high mantelshelf. This observation had saved them from mobilizing the kitchen staff at ten o'clock at night to search the house for them.

The Miracle of Moon Crescent [19] is the tale of how a man disappeared from a locked room only to re-appear, dead, hanging from a tree outside the building. As no explanation was forthcoming, it was put down to spiritual powers, until Father Brown enlightened them. Neither holy or unholy angels had done the deed, he told them, it was the act of wicked men unaided by spiritual powers. He said he knew something about Satanism, which horrified the innocent with things half-understood and made children's flesh creep. This explained why Satanism was so fond of mysteries, initiations, secret societies and all the rest of it but however grand and grave it looked it always hid a small, mad smile.

The seed for this story was probably sown one afternoon at

a gathering in the drawing room at St John's when Father O'Connor began to hold forth about the Black Mass, its exponents and its history and finished by talking about Aleister Crowley, whose *Confessions* was on his bookshelves, and Satanism. Mrs Steinthal caused a minor sensation when she looked up from her needlework and casually mentioned that a Satanist had been to tea at the house just a few weeks ago. The woman had been to Bradford in search of likely candidates, had found one, and was taking her to Bristol to be trained. Father O'Connor and Chesterton were keen to learn more but unfortunately Mrs Steinthal had no further information.

When Chesterton had lunch with Father O'Connor in Heckmondwike, the priest happened to mention that, after forty years of deliberation, the use of the planchette had been condemned by the Catholic Church. Chesterton then admitted he had used the planchette regularly at one time, but had to stop because of ensuing bad headaches at the back of his head. These were followed by what we would now describe as a hangover and with what Chesterton described as a 'bad smell in the mind'.[20] This was the beginning of despair, the priest told him, and we must never abandon our will to an unknown power as there is no guarantee it will be beneficent. The wicked men in *The Miracle of Moon Crescent* were wicked indeed, but not wicked enough to be dealing with spiritual powers.

'Father Brown was not very fond of the telephone. He was one who preferred to watch people's faces and feel social atmospheres, and he knew well that without these things, verbal messages are apt to be very misleading, especially from total strangers.' Father Brown's dislike of the telephone is described in *The Insoluble Problem*,[21] a dislike shared by Father O'Connor, as the artist Stanley Parker discovered to his cost when trying to arrange an interview with the priest. Stanley Parker, a young Australian artist, was in the West Riding to interview and sketch the local worthies for national publications such as *The Tatler* and *The Illustrated Sporting and Dramatic News*. Father O'Connor was in good company; other personalities in the area to come under the artist's scrutiny included J. B. Priestley, Lord Bingley of Bramham Park and Lord Harewood of Harewood House.

Stanley Parker thought it was 'delightfully quaint'[22] when he first discovered that the priest disliked modern amenities, in fact he didn't own a wireless set either but would go into his curate's room if there was anything he wanted to hear especially! After making three wasted visits to the presbytery, Parker no longer thought the lack of the telephone quaint but 'positively medieval'.[23] At last, during a violent snowstorm, the presbytery door was opened and the artist was confronted by 'the rubicund figure of Chesterton's Father Brown'.[24] Parker immediately forgave the lack of a telephone when he found himself face to face with such 'a beloved character of fiction';[25] he felt as if he were about sit down to tea with Pickwick, or had bumped into Falstaff on the bus. The artist came to the conclusion that he would 'willingly have walked through a dozen snowstorms for the privilege of shaking hands with him'.[26] It seems Chesterton had not disguised Father O'Connor enough to deceive those who had met his alter ego.

Father O'Connor was parish priest at St Cuthbert's at this time and his own small room must have made quite a contrast to the stately homes of some of Parker's subjects. He described the room as being warm, cosy and overcrowded with books piled everywhere and pictures covering every available inch of the walls. On the mantelpiece he spotted one of his own drawings. Boxes of cigars and packets of incense topped every piece of furniture and there were the brown paper parcels, tantalizingly half-open. The conversation ranged over a wide spectrum and as he rambled on the artist thought sometimes his subject was half-asleep, but noted he kept a watchful eye on what was taking place. The drawing completed, Father O'Connor showed Parker some of his art collection including a large oil painting by Turner, and some tiny studies on scraps of canvas no bigger than a postcard which Turner used to give as tips to his caretaker. When he finally left, Father O'Connor told him to call again sometime, adding 'I'm afraid you can't ring as I'm not on the 'phone.'[27] As he walked down the path, the artist thought once more that this was 'delightfully quaint'.[28]

Chesterton considered the Father Brown stories more a way of paying bills rather than as great literature and when informed that his bank balance needed increasing, he would dash off another tale from notes scribbled on the back of an envelope. Neither was Father O'Connor impressed with them, at least on his first reading, but put this down to an unfamiliarity with the genre. Many years later, after re-reading them, he declared himself amazed at their ingenuity and the dexterity of the workmanship. He always felt though that Father Brown was rather too deft and artistic in his solutions but he would have been delighted to solve them the same way himself, instead he found himself as puzzled as everyone else before all was revealed.

Father Brown's fame sped around the world, in spite of some critics being less than complimentary, and Father O'Connor was surprised to meet Spaniards and Czech-Slovaks to whom he was familiar. Recognition, however, could sometimes lead to uncomfortable situations with folk unable to distinguish between the real and fictional characters. Others would be unduly reticent or be on their guard in case the priest became the detective. On one occasion, Father O'Connor was introduced at a local bookshop to a smart young man who happened to be an international crook who disappeared, along with his confederate, less than twenty-four hours later. The man had reason to be on his guard, as he had been obtaining rare books from a London bookseller via the American Consulate in Bradford. In conversation with Father O'Connor he pretended to know Mrs Alice Meynell, the poet, and others with whom the priest was familiar and who began to realize that in fact the young man didn't know them at all. The London bookseller was warned, but not before the thief had escaped with two hundred pounds' worth of books.

Father O'Connor was first portrayed in a film, made in the USA in 1934: *Father Brown, Detective,* with Walter Connolly in the title role and Paul Lukas as Flambeau. Father O'Connor was delighted with the news and approved the selection of the actor in the title role. Unfortunately, he died just two years before Alec Guinness portrayed Father Brown in a British film, with Peter Finch as Flambeau. In his autobiography, Alec Guinness described how, during the making the film, events so conspired against his strong anti-Romanism views that they led to his eventual reception into the Catholic Church in 1956.

The actor's strong anti-clericalism was reduced by his friendship with the Anglo-Catholic Revd Cyril Tomkinson but his anti-Romanism remained until an incident occurred during the filming of *Father Brown*. Taking a break during night-shooting in Burgundy, Guinness, still in costume, took a stroll along the road to the village. A young boy called out, ran after him, took his hand and kept up excited non-stop chatter until he suddenly wished him 'Bonsoir, mon père!'[29] before dashing off to his home. The actor had not dared utter a word in case his excruciating French scared the child but as he continued his walk he reflected that a Church which inspired such confidence in a child, and made even its unknown priests so easily approachable, could not be as scheming and creepy as so often made out. Slowly he began to shake off his long-taught, long-absorbed prejudices. Could it be that the 'real' Father Brown's spirit was pushing events along?

Alec Guinness's son was seriously ill just before filming started and, when his future looked doubtful, his father developed the habit of dropping into a nearby Catholic church on his way home to think and find peace. He made a bargain with God that, if his son recovered and later wished to become a Catholic, he would not stop him. At the time this sounded to him like a supreme sacrifice. His son did recover and when they moved house he found the only public school was Catholic. Recalling his promise he sent his boy to the school and, sure enough, he eventually became a Catholic. His father, meanwhile, seeing how events were going, decided to stay as a guest at a Trappist monastery, taking his researches to the extreme. It may not have had the expected or even desired effect, as Alec Guinness was received into the Church and 'felt he had come home'.[30]

Thirteen Father Brown stories were adapted for British television in 1974, starring Kenneth More in the title role. The first episode was 'The Hammer of God' from the *Innocence of Father Brown,* as were a further three. There were four stories from *The Incredulity*; three from *The Secret*; and one each from

The Scandal and *The Wisdom of Father Brown*. The first Father Brown story, *The Blue Cross*, was not used but the second, *The Secret Garden,* finished the series.

Notes

1. Chesterton, *Autobiography*, p. 326.
2. 'Father Brown', *Father Brown*, BBC script, papers of John O'Connor.
3. Chesterton, *Autobiography*, p. 327.
4. Ibid., p. 328.
5. Ibid., p. 323.
6. Ibid.
7. Ibid.
8. Ibid.
9. Ibid.
10. Ibid.
11. O'Connor, *Brief Chronicle*, BBC script, papers of John O'Connor.
12. O'Connnor, *Father Brown on Chesterton*, p. 39.
13. Chesterton, *Complete Father Brown Stories*, p. 23.
14. Ibid., p. 64.
15. Ibid., p. 265.
16. Ibid., p. 269.
17. Chesterton, 'A Note on Father Brown', *The Heaton Review*.
18. Chesterton, *Complete Father Brown Stories*, p. 660.
19. Ibid., p. 368.
20. O'Connor, *Father Brown on Chesterton*, p. 74.
21. Chesterton, *Complete Father Brown Stories*, p. 691.
22. Parker, 'Monsignor John O'Connor', *Yorkshire Observer*.
23. Ibid.
24. Ibid.
25. Ibid.
26. Ibid.
27. Ibid.
28. Ibid.
29. Guinness, *Blessings in Disguise*, p. 36.
30. Ibid., p. 38.

Chapter 6

1919–52: Model Parish Priest

Father O'Connor's new parish of St Cuthbert's was one of two halves, the rich and the poor. In one half lived the rich in their large detached houses, surrounded by gardens. These were the homes of merchants and mill owners, doctors and lawyers, jewellers and car manufacturers, some of them Catholic.

In the other half lived the poor in their 'back-to-backs' in the mean streets huddled around the huge mill where many of them worked, or often didn't during the Depression. These were long terraces of houses with one or two rooms upstairs and one down, a 'cellar-head' kitchen, that is a tiny kitchen at the top of the cellar steps, and an outside toilet. Identical houses adjoined the backs of them, reached by a passage between them. Many of the families housed here were Irish Catholic immigrants. The two halves of the parish were joined by Wilmer Road, with St Cuthbert's church in the centre, its parish priest equally welcome and equally comfortable in the homes in either half.

Father James Lahart, one-time parish priest of First Martyr's church, considered Father O'Connor an exemplar to all priests who used his many gifts and graces to influence, guide and mould the souls in his care in the Christian way of life. Among his attributes was tremendous grace in the presence of the sick and infirm and joy among little ones, which Father Lahart thought sprang from an essentially simple faith based on the love of Christ and Our Lady and founded on prayer.

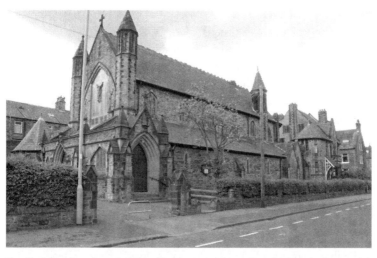

St Cuthbert's church, Bradford, exterior. Fr O'Connor's parish 1919–52.

Father Thomas Keegan, who together with Father Thomas Maudslay was appointed curate to Father O'Connor in 1946, just six years before the latter's death, echoed these observations of his parish priest who was never known to miss his prayers and who struggled to read his Office even in the last days of his life. When I visited Father Keegan at Sheffield, where he was living in retirement, he told me that it was Father O'Connor's conversation that he remembered mostly. He would talk incessantly and over lunch, which could last for hours, they would discuss the current topic of news, to which their parish priest was always able to supply any necessary background information. The only time he did stop talking was when a curate returned from holiday; after supper he would visit their room, put a bottle of whisky on the table, sit back and say 'tell me about it'. Father Keegan recalled how good it was to come back full of the holiday and be able to do just that while Father O'Connor listened quietly for once.

I was fortunate to be able to speak to a number of ex-parishioners who remembered their parish priest as being short and round like a barrel with highly polished cheeks, which seems not too far removed from his fictional counterpart. Unlike Father Brown, however, Father O'Connor was often to be seen, dressed in a dark leather-belted raincoat, with great gauntlets on his hands and a 'deerstalker kind of thing' on his head, riding his motorbike around his parish. Past students of St Joseph's Catholic College for Girls remembered how he roared up to the college on it, much to the amazement of any student seeing him for the first time. Nor did he stick to clerical black. At a time when all priests conformed to the code, he was happy to don a grey suit, and was not averse to wearing a Yorkshire flat cap with it. In the environs of his church he could be seen wearing a biretta, but even this was not usual in England.

Priests and parishioners agreed that Father O'Connor never did what was usual; being one of a kind, years ahead of his time and while not exactly a rebel, being 'antipathetic to the minutiae of the law' and not averse to bending the very rigid rules if he felt the occasion demanded it. Father Keegan recalled that almost everything brought in by the Second Vatican Council Father O'Connor had privately introduced himself years before.

Outdoor collections were made around the parish on Friday nights and Saturday mornings and the two curates at St Cuthbert's took a half each but avoided certain houses. These were always visited by the parish priest himself, who would say he had to go and do his outdoor collecting, to which the curates would reply 'of course you have' but knowing this was his excuse to visit his old cronies! One such family recalled how he would open the door, walk straight in and call 'God save all here present' before entertaining them with a song as they consumed their usual Friday night fish and chips. Often he had tea at the home of two maiden ladies, always two boiled eggs with bread and butter, though in wartime when eggs were no longer available it had to be dried egg powder, scrambled. This was followed with a smoke of either his favourite pipe or a box of cigars he kept on their sideboard. If Father O'Connor lit a cigar when he visited them, his parishioners knew they were in for a long session as the butt of his cigar would go into his pipe, or he would put a pin through to it to enable him to smoke it to the very end. He was very fond of this pastime and he was so bad-tempered when he gave it up for Lent that his curates asked the bishop to tell him to re-start! His evening would often finish at the 'posh' end of the parish with a visit to the home of his non-Catholic friend Sir Anthony Gadie. He was one of the most influential public men in the city at that time, a Conservative city councillor and one-time Lord Mayor, not to mention a leading Freemason. That they were almost complete opposites would not deter Father O'Connor, indeed it would add to the attraction.

Father O'Connor was known for his great love of the poor, many of whom lived 'behind t' mill'. The mill around which so many of St Cuthbert's parishioners lived and worked, was Lister's Mill, after its owner, Samuel Cunliffe Lister, the most important textile inventor of his time. Built in an Italianate style, the floor space covered twenty-seven acres, one shed alone being a quarter of a mile long. The 250-foot-high chimney still dominates the city skyline, though the mill has now been converted into very expensive apartments. The mill was the largest silk factory in Europe and employed 11,000 people making a range of fabrics, but it was most famous for the silk velvet produced there. 1,000 yards of it was used at George V's coronation but much of it would hang as curtains in the homes of the local rich textile manufacturers and merchants. When Father O'Connor paid his Friday visit to the poor families whose members worked there, he would be giving rather than collecting and many of them regarded 'generosity' as his second name.

One sprightly elderly lady recalled how her proud young mother of four insisted on paying her sixpence each Friday night, even though both she and her husband needed to work in the mill, and how Father O'Connor would always find ways of seeing it came back to them one way or another. When the father was very ill, for instance, the priest sent the children to the corner shop where to their surprise, and subsequently to their parents' surprise, a large hamper of food awaited them, paid for by the weekly sixpences their priest had collected.

Father O'Connor was not only generous with money and gifts but, equally important, also with his time having the great ability of making whoever he was with feel that they had been singled out for his special attention. What this lady didn't know was how many other families had felt they too had been singled out for his special attention and had benefited in similar ways. When a family of nine, for example, with an out-of-work invalid father at its head, moved into the parish just before Christmas, they expected to have a very frugal time. Instead they were able to feast on the largest goose they had ever seen when they opened a parcel that appeared on their doorstep – Father O'Connor's way of welcoming them to the parish!

With his love of children and of the poor, it is no surprise that poor children came in for plenty of special attention from Father O'Connor, but again in subtle rather than obvious ways. One rather less poor child noticed during Sunday school, which he always conducted, that the poorer children were always given the first opportunity of answering his questions. She gradually realized that this was because a right answer produced the reward of one penny, which the child could spend immediately after at the sweetie shop around the corner. As there would normally not be enough money in the

A christening at St Cuthbert's church, Bradford, 10 September 1931.

family for sweets, and one penny could buy two kinds of sweets for a half-penny each, this was a real Sunday treat for the child.

One of Father O'Connor's forward-thinking innovations was the introduction of face-to-face confession, at least for the children who found the traditional dark wooden confessional box very scary. He would open the door on his side of the box and have the child kneel in front of him, his cloak enclosing their two heads as he heard their confession. If there was a big queue for confession and the children were talking too loudly, he would take them off to a bench at the back of church. An ex-altar boy recalled that as they got older, some of the boys would stomp to the confessional trying to sound like an adult in order to slip anonymously into the box. This was not always a successful ploy for, at the end of confession, Father O'Connor would ask 'How's your dad?' or something similar, showing he still knew perfectly well whose confession he was hearing. It was no good waiting to confess to one of the curates either as they were under orders to open their doors to the children. This innovation had at least one unfortunate consequence. Noticing the practice, a lady new to the parish assumed this was the custom for all and knelt solemnly at the priest's feet. Father O'Connor politely heard her confession but didn't embarrass her by referring to her mistake, the embarrassment came later when her friends enlightened her!

Father O'Connor believed strongly in the power of healing, through prayer, through a blessing and through the Sacrament of Extreme Unction, which he didn't reserve solely for those in danger of death, being happy to anoint something as minor as a painful toothache. It was the norm in the parish to ask him for healing and interviewees have cited cases of his blessing curing anything from eczema to fits. His great faith in the help to be obtained by the intercession of Our Lady is illustrated by the story of a Polish couple who had fled the country during the war, becoming separated in so doing. The man found himself in Bradford and thinking Father O'Connor may know of other Poles who might help he went to visit him. The priest sent him instead to pray at the Shrine of Our Lady at Walsingham, in

Norfolk. The only other person in the chapel was a nurse from a hospital at a nearby American airbase and as they left they began chatting together. He told the nurse his story and at the end of it she asked his name. On hearing it she told him to go with her to the hospital, where she reunited him with his wife. Back in Bradford he went to thank Father O'Connor, who showed no surprise whatever at the outcome.

Father O'Connor did not always exude sweetness and light, and was as famous for his bad language, first encountered at the Franciscan academy, as he was for his good works, as one lady discovered after knocking on the presbytery door one night. She had called to complain about the bad language of the Irish navvies re-surfacing the road outside the church. He

St Cuthbert's presbytery, where Fr O'Connor had his room and through whose door many famous people entered.

agreed with her, not entirely as she might have hoped, when he said 'Yes, they're buggers aren't they?'

Neither did Father O'Connor suffer fools gladly and his choir often got the sharp end his tongue. Being a lover of great music, he didn't always appreciate their attempts and past choristers recalled how he was quite likely to turn from the altar and demand they 'stop that bloody row' as he wasn't able to concentrate on the Mass. The altar servers also were often on the receiving end of some rough treatment, but when one of them had a long and serious illness and was reading a book a day, Father O'Connor came every day with a new one for him, not a serious religious tome but a good 'boys' book'. Even the headmaster of one of the Catholic schools came in for criticism when he assisted at Mass, being told loud enough for all to hear, 'You know Charlie, every time you come on this altar you make a bugger of things.' But it was said without malice and with a twinkle in his eye.

Father O'Connor had a rather surprising piece of advice for one of his altar boys who was going off to train for the priesthood at Ushaw College, Durham but first he gave him a packet of forty sixpences, worth one pound, and the blessing for someone undertaking a long journey. Durham was not very far away, thought the young man, but later realized Father O'Connor was speaking, of course, about his journey through life. He then told him that at the seminary there would be lots of things that he had to do, and lots of things he hadn't to do, and if he did the things that he had to do, and didn't do the things he hadn't to do, they would make him a bishop and he would be 'no bloody good'. To come out with such an unexpected remark to a fifteen-year-old going off to the seminary was typical of the priest known to him as Johnny. As he is now a retired priest, he may well have followed the advice as did Johnny himself, as neither became a bishop. It is said of people who are blunt and to the point, that they are not afraid to 'call a spade, a spade'. Yorkshire folk are considered to go even further, daring to call a spade 'a bloody shovel'. Father O'Connor was a true Yorkshireman in this respect.

Father O'Connor's language was not moderated when he

visited St Joseph's College for Girls, as many of them
remembered. Sister Joseph was no doubt surprised when,
during an English lesson, the priest asked her if she was
familiar with the poem beginning 'A wonderful bird is the
Pelican'. When she replied in the negative, he continued 'its
beak can hold more than its belly can, its beak can hold enough
for a week, and I wonder how the hell it can'.

Sister Joseph might have expected something in a more
serious vein when Father O'Connor brought his friend Hilaire
Belloc, whose poetry the girls had been studying, to visit the
Sixth Form. The School Captain asked him to recite for them,
perhaps *Duncton Hill* which they all knew by heart, but Belloc
said he couldn't recite serious poetry so would give them
instead something which had the merit of brevity:

> To see how much petrol was left in the tank,
> A match was ignited by Timothy Hall,
> And except for the money he had in the bank,
> His unfortunate widow got nothing at all!

Father O'Connor's first meeting with Hilaire Belloc was
arranged by their mutual friend, Robert Hudson, who invited
them both to dinner in London. They became firm friends, with
Belloc becoming a familiar visitor at the presbytery and the
college. Previously he had stayed with Father O'Connor at
Heckmondwike, coming on one occasion direct from a visit to
Ireland and departing on the night train to London to resign his
seat in Parliament. When Belloc's daughter, Elizabeth, was a
guest at St Cuthbert's presbytery in 1941, Father O'Connor
was not able to sidestep the ever-present Brontë sisters as
Elizabeth was to address the girls of St Joseph's College on
Wuthering Heights, Emily Brontë's violent novel of love and
passion on the high moors of Haworth. Hilaire, himself, had
always admired the novel but had never visited Brontë country
so he was pleased that Elizabeth had been able to visit the
Brontë parsonage, only a few miles away and now part of the
Bradford Metropolitan District. Whether Father O'Connor was
obliged to go with her we don't know. As he told his daughter

in a letter, Belloc considered Father O'Connor to be one of the most intelligent men he had ever met and 'wonderfully alive to everything'[1] and was very happy that he had been able to accommodate her at the presbytery.

Father O'Connor took a keen interest in education and was a frequent, and welcome, visitor at both the lower and upper schools, and many pupils have fond memories of those days. He paid his weekly visit to the primary school on Friday mornings, a visit looked forward to by the children as he always had an interesting story to tell. Later he attempted teaching the older children to sing, but they didn't think they ever came up to his exacting standards.

He was likely to turn up at St Joseph's College at any time of the day, usually to talk to the Sixth Formers on English poetry, French carols, Latin authors, his travels abroad, or a point of theology. Of course his theories on the latter subject were more in keeping with post-Vatican II, than his own times. When the school library was opened Father O'Connor donated many valuable books, while pictures from his own art collection hung on the walls of the college. He would discuss the appreciation of art and music, rather than theory, with the girls, on one occasion reading them a paper he had given at a Conference of Higher Studies at Cambridge, pleading for the culture of the emotions. Having talked about art, he would take them across the road to the Cartwright Hall Art Gallery in Lister Park to look at the paintings.

Often Father O'Connor would arrive at the college with one of his famous friends in tow, giving the girls a glimpse of a world they might otherwise never have known while at the same time giving substance to some of the topics discussed. In 1922, the Jesuit priest and theologian Revd C. C. Martindale, gave a lecture on psycho-analysis and on St Paul's life and work on a later visit. Dom Gregory Ould was charmed on his visit with the choir's interpretation of Chesterton's *Nativity* which he had set to music.

Music also featured when Father O'Connor brought along Sir Richard Terry, the musicologist, organist and director of music at Westminster Cathedral, whom the girls had met at the

Father O'Connor with Sir Richard Terry and Miss Hodgkinson at
St Joseph's College, 1931.

Wharfedale Festival of Music at Ilkley where Sir Richard was
a judge. He had praised the singing of their choirs and been
delighted with the junior choir's rendering of *The Walrus and
the Carpenter.* On one of his visits to the college, he
accompanied Father O'Connor as he sang a selection of Basque
carols, some of which he had contributed to a collection of folk
carols edited by Sir Richard. It was said that to hear him sing
his translation of *O Bethlehem,* a carol of great pathos and
beauty, was not an experience soon forgotten, in a good way I
think! Father O'Connor also contributed a number of hymns to
the Westminster Hymnal edited by Sir Richard.

Father O'Connor was again persuaded to sing a French song
when he visited the college with the actress, Dorothy
Holmes-Gore, before she entertained the girls herself with
music and singing. Several of the senior students watched her
performance the following evening in the title role of St Joan in
George Bernard Shaw's play being performed at the Bradford
Alhambra. The priest later brought along Bernard Merefield,
who was the Bishop of Amiens in the same play, to entertain

the girls with songs and selections played on the piano.

Robert Speaight[2] thought Father O'Connor seemed to have strayed into his presbytery from the Irish music hall, especially when lying back in his chair singing some popular song. He considered his friend's cheerful, round-faced and rubicund simplicity, deceptive, and that it hid the folk wisdom in his blood and many other kinds of wisdom in his brain. Speaight was yet another actor taken along to meet Father O'Connor's Sixth Form girls when he was appearing as Thomas à Becket in T. S. Eliot's play *Murder in the Cathedral,* at the Leeds Grand Theatre.

Much excitement was generated when, in 1926, senior and junior choirs were asked to sing at St George's Hall, where G. K. Chesterton was to address the annual meeting of the Bradford branch of the Roman Catholic Women's League. None of them had ever seen him and speculation was rife, the burning question being what he was like. In a short piece entitled 'GKC Anticipated' in the school magazine for 1926, hopes were expressed that Father O'Connor would bring the great man to the college the following morning, the Sixth were especially hoping they would have a private audience with him in their room. Excitement fairly leaps from the page as they consider what such a visit would mean and what a tale they would have to tell to their grandchildren. They envisaged him stepping from a car, enveloped in a coat with a large fur collar and a small trilby hat!

The following piece in the magazine, entitled *GKC Realized,* told how it really happened. Chesterton was greeted with a storm of applause from the huge crowd when he took the stage at St George's Hall, the College girls bemoaned the fact that their clapping was muffled by their white gloves. GK did not hitch up his coat or cough deeply, as anticipated, but played with his ring, twirled his moustache, and twined each separate lock of hair around his finger as he held his audience spellbound for fifty minutes. The choir sang *Puer Natus,* translated by Father O'Connor, and performed for the first time Dom Gregory Ould's setting of Chesterton's poem *The Nativity.* Father O'Connor gave the vote of thanks referring to

GK's continuous expansion. With applause from the man himself and laughter from the audience, he hastened to explain he meant his mental expansion as well as the physical.

A hint was given on leaving that the girls might expect a school visit from GKC time permitting. On Monday morning they were relieved to hear the sound of a car approaching and then to see alighting from the car, 'with all the appearance of an English man-of-war taking a Spanish galleon out for an airing', as one girl put it, were Father O'Connor and Mr Chesterton. The latter was not wearing a large fur collar or a small trilby but 'his apparel bespoke the man of genius, who refuses to subscribe to the tyranny of fashion'. He was very tall and wore an ample coat and comfortable scarf while, with a quaint-shaped hat which topped a shock of hair turning grey, together with his pince-nez, he gave every indication of being the personification of good humour. There was much speculation as to the identity of the young man driving the car, son, secretary, chauffeur? None of these but his host a Mr Fattorini, probably the nineteen-year-old Edward William, son of John Enrico Fattorini, founder, in 1912 in Bradford, of Grattan, which became one the UK's leading mail order catalogue companies.

The Sixth Form were treated to a private reading by Chesterton of his poem, *Elegy in a Country Churchyard,* before they met the remaining staff and pupils in the school hall. They sang the school song for him, words by Father O'Connor with music by Dom Alphege Shebbeare, before he recited a couple of Belloc's *Cautionary Tales.*

There was some consternation as the visitors left. As Mr Fattorini took the steering wheel of the small car, it was feared he would be engulfed by his passengers as both Father O'Connor and Chesterton climbed into the 'dicky' seat. They left to the hearty cheers and clapping of the whole school.

St Joseph's College began life as a private school in 1905 and moved to the present Cunliffe Road premises, opposite Lister Park, in 1908. Celebrations on the occasion of the Silver Jubilee took place over two days, beginning with Pontifical High Mass in the school grounds, sung by the Bishop of Leeds,

Dr Cowgill, and followed by a banquet with the Lord and Lady Mayoress, civic and educational representatives. Father O'Connor proposed the toast to the bishop following that to the Lord Mayor and City Council. His speech was, as expected, full of fun. 'I am glad the City Council have been faithfully dealt with', he said, 'because I have just had a summons for my gas bill, and I feel I could not impart into my remarks that note of geniality which ought to prevail on such occasions.'[3] Laughter again erupted from his audience as he told the tale of the man taken to the opera by a woman to hear *Tristan*. She talked incessantly through the three-hour performance after which she asked if he was coming with her to *Parsifal*. 'Oh, yes', he replied, 'I've never heard you in *Parsifal!*'[4] On a more serious note, Father O'Connor as MC for the day, gave Solemn Benediction.

The British National Opera Company made an annual visit to Bradford, and Father O'Connor was likely to arrive at the college with tickets for the Sixth Formers. One girl he treated to the best seat at the opera as a reward for her good acting in a difficult part in the Prize Day play, others he took to a recital by a famous pianist. Feast Day was often the time for a trek across the moors to Ilkley, led by Father O'Connor, with lunch provided before returning home by train. 'Carriage Day', carriages being later replaced by 'charabancs', was the final function before the students left for university. These would again be led by Father O'Connor, usually to one of Yorkshire's beautiful abbeys or convents where he was sure to have old friends ready to greet them.

St Bede's was the Grammar School for boys, where Father O'Connor was the first assistant master with Revd Dr Hinsley as Headmaster, as previously mentioned. In 1918, the school moved from Drewton Street to Heaton Hall and its adjacent estate, close to St Cuthbert's church, with the present school being built on the site and opening in 1939. Father O'Connor maintained his interest in the school, being on the Board of Governors for many years and making an annual donation to their funds, an amount in excess of the school fees for a year. He was generous as ever, not only with money, but also with gifts which included a mosaic of Our Lady and a Flemish carving of the Ascension, the day on which St Bede died.

He regularly attended the Old Boys' Association Annual Dinner at the Belle Vue Hotel. An account in *St Bede's Magazine* in February 1922, praises his lecture, at the dinner the previous December, on Browning's *Bishop Blougram's Apology,* after which the Old Boys plied him with questions on a variety of subjects. These ranged from the Church in Spain to Modern Foreign Policy, and though both his patience and learning were tested, neither gave way, for which they gave additional thanks.

Eric Gill was Father O'Connor's guest at the Old Boys' dinner on more than one occasion. 'Ye Bille of ye Fare', in a font unavailable on my laptop, still exists for this 'Feaste' to which they went on 31 January 1925. Following the description of each course is an appropriate literary quotation. The wine list included one claret, one burgundy, two sauternes, and no less than four champagnes, the most expensive being the Veuve Cliquot at twenty-five shillings a bottle, the cheapest just five shillings for the St Julien claret.

On one of the Carriage Day outings, Father O'Connor took the Sixth Form ladies of St Joseph's College to the Bar Convent at York, another educational establishment in which he took a great interest, for lunch with Revd Mother. He was well known at the convent where he always dined with other clergy before attending the annual Speech Day and prize-giving. Unlike the other clergy he always stayed overnight and next day would give a talk which was much appreciated by the girls, especially when he was generous in praise of their singing or dramatic performances of the previous evening.

In December 1936, their dramatic performance was *A Mystery Play in honour of The Nativity of Our Lord,* by R. H. Benson which had been written originally for the Order's Cambridge foundation (Institute of the Blessed Virgin Mary). Father O'Connor was not at all impressed by the play and though it had been well acted he thought it hadn't really been worth the effort. Speech Day 1932, saw the first performance of the Bar Convent school song written by Father O'Connor, with music by Dom Alphege Shebbeare, to replace an older one. The song recalled the legend of St Michael who came to the Sisters' rescue when they were besieged by a fanatical mob in the seventeenth century.

A student writing in the Bar Convent School Magazine in 1934 compared Father O'Connor's talks to a gold rush; there would be plenty of nuggets but it was necessary to sift and search for them. In describing his talks as 'different' , the girl was, she believed, paying him the highest tribute of the present age. Father O'Connor's Sunday sermons were also 'different'. During the Second World War he could be extremely outspoken about the enemy one week but the following week be just as eloquent on the merits, or lack of merit, of a book he had read during the week. Many people, both Catholic and non-Catholic, appreciated these sermons to the extent of persuading him to publish a selection which he did in 1940, under the title *A Month of Sundays, the Foolishness of Father Brown*. In the Introduction, which he signed 'All that is left of Father Brown', he expressed a wish that they may be of value to those in a similar situation to himself, namely 'Poor over-faced fellows whose whole solicitude in the pulpit is not to repeat the sins of their youth and their ignorances, nor yet to reproduce tant bien que mal, the well-pondered learning and zeal of others.'[5]

As the convent student found when listening to his talks, the sermons often produced a golden nugget, or a 'sound-bite' as they would probably be termed nowadays. One that tends to leap out is that 'Protestants are so often better than their religion, but Catholics are seldom as good as theirs.'[6] On Christian marriage he wrote that 'Parties should be of a common faith. Perfect mutual love and honesty may get on without, but they are handicapped by not having the same motive for their sacred thoughts.'[7] But he also advised his parishioners against attacking any denomination as such, rather they should imitate Jesus Christ in so far as 'He never says a word against false religion, only against false piety'.[8] This was something that Father O'Connor not only preached but practised, both with his Protestant or non-religious friends, and with the non-Catholic partners of his parishioners whom he treated with the same care and concern.

It was some time after the first collection of Chesterton's *Father Brown* stories appeared in the bookshops that most of his parishioners realized he was based on their beloved parish priest, and they knew little, if anything, of what he got up to when away from his parish.

Notes

1. Belloc, *Letter*, 29 July 1941.
2. Speaight, *The Life of Eric Gill*, p. 180.
3. *Leeds Mercury*, 20 July 1933.
4. Ibid.
5. O'Connor, *Month of Sundays*, Introduction.
6. Ibid., p. 25.
7. Ibid., p. 22.
8. Ibid., p. 8.

Chapter 7

The 1920s: The Ditchling Years

Eric Gill was familiar with St Cuthbert's church before Father O'Connor became its parish priest as this was where he worshipped when he visited his friend Charles Rutherston. Charles, who had Anglicized his name, was a member of the Rothenstein family whose father Moritz, a German merchant, had opened his Bradford warehouse in 1859. Unlike his artist brothers, Albert Rutherston, who had also Anglicized his name, and William Rothenstein, who hadn't, Charles went into the family business and stayed in Bradford all his life. William became Principal of the Royal College of Art, in London, and his son, John, of whom more later, was born there. Moritz, and his wife Bertha Rothenstein, are buried in the Jewish section of the same cemetery in Bradford as Father O'Connor himself, and it was the carving of their grave headstone that brought Eric Gill to Bradford.

In January 1919, Eric Gill and Hilary Pepler stayed with Father O'Connor at the Church of the Holy Spirit in Heckmondwike. The following day all three went to Bradford to visit Father Blessing at St Joseph's church before Gill and Pepler travelled on to Edinburgh. Later the same year, on 2 July, Father O'Connor moved to St Cuthbert's and it was not long before he was putting his own stamp on it, ably abetted by his friend Eric who was an early guest at the presbytery.

Soon after his conversion to Catholicism in 1913, Eric Gill had carved the famous set of the Stations of the Cross for

Westminster Cathedral in London; now Father O'Connor
decided he would like a similar set for his church. Not only
that, he had expressed an interest in a crucifix Gill had recently
sold at the Goupil Gallery and suggested Gill carve him one in
olive wood. Oh! And he would also like statues of Our Lady
and St Joseph. Gill was pleased when his estimate of £350 for
his Stations of the Cross was confirmed but Father O'Connor's
other suggestions had to remain as such for some time. In fact
Gill never did get around to carving St Joseph and this has led
to much speculation as to who did carve the statue in St
Cuthbert's. Eventually I was able to solve the mystery but more
of that later. Father O'Connor fared better with his request for
a stone relief of St Anthony, for the sum of £40, which Gill
started in December 1919 and finished the following February.

Eric Gill and Hilary Pepler came to Bradford from
Hawkesyard Priory in March 1920 after their profession as
Dominican tertiaries. The Third Order of St Dominic is a lay
Order, the First and Second Orders being for friars and nuns
respectively, whose members live a normal life, but one which
revolves around Christ, in daily Mass, the Liturgy of the Hours
and the rosary. Gill was now living at Hopkins Crank on
Ditchling Common, two miles north of the village in West
Sussex where he had lived after leaving London. His friend,
Hilary Pepler, was a craftsman-printer who had set up his
printing press at Sopers, the house in Ditchling village vacated
by Gill. He had accompanied Gill to Hawkesyard Priory in
March 1917 where both had given a lecture. Pepler, a Quaker,
had long talks while he was there with the Prior, Father Vincent
McNabb, and was impressed enough to begin taking instruction
from the parish priest on their return to Ditchling. Father
Vincent visited them over the summer, and, after a Retreat at
Hawkesyard in October, Hilary Pepler was received into the
Catholic Church, his wife following him some seven years later.

Pepler now moved to Ditchling Common, to Hallets about a
quarter of a mile from Hopkins Crank. He installed his printing
press in a nearby reconditioned farm building and re-named it the
St Dominic's Press. By early 1918, Gill, though never officially
demobilized, had managed to leave the war behind and get back

to work on the Westminster Stations of the Cross where he was interrupted on 5 April by Desmond Chute with whom he talked for almost three hours. Desmond Macready Chute was a Catholic from birth and educated at Downside School. He went on to study sculpture at the Slade, though his background was in the theatre. After this long first conversation in the cathedral, Chute was soon visiting Ditchling regularly and within a couple of weeks he found himself carving stone for Eric and being taken into the household.

The three of them, Gill, Pepler and Chute, 'formed a sort of society of three'[1] with 'the idea of a guild or company of craftsmen who should be united not merely by a common desire to further the interests of their work but by common acceptance of a rule or way of life'.[2] With Desmond Chute, himself a member of the Third Order of St Francis, on board and Gill and Pepler becoming more drawn to Father Vincent, it was decided that, rather than establishing a completely new rule of life, they would become Dominican tertiaries.

Gill considered that God had shown his affection for him by his choice of those he sent to befriend him after his conversion. Three friends to whom he felt he owed everything were literarily a godsend at this time, Desmond Chute, who later became a priest; Father Vincent McNabb of Hawkesyard and Father John O'Connor of Heckmondwike. Gill considered the two priests 'were in a manner of speaking my spiritual mother and father', while their minds were 'in the very first rank of noble minds . . .'.[3] Gill was even closer to Desmond Chute who now worked with him on a daily basis. He was able to share his ideas and difficulties with him and felt able to talk to him without shame or reserve, Chute being the only person to take precedence over Father O'Connor as Gill's confidante. A worldly-wise friend and counsellor, with the same way of thinking, Father O'Connor was a great help to the community at Ditchling. When Jacques Maritain's philosophy first came to their notice it was to Father O'Connor that they turned to undertake the translation of Maritain's book, *Art et Scholastique*, a book which they came to read on an almost daily basis.

Father O'Connor continued to get himself established in his new parish, not least by having Gill engrave a St Cuthbert's cross as the logo for his letterheading. The proposed Stations of the Cross were top of the agenda when Gill and Pepler came to Bradford in March 1920, but it was for coffee and cigars at a café close to the railway station that Father O'Connor conducted them when they first arrived. The three of them spent the following day at the Bradford Arts Club, of which Father O'Connor was a member, where there was an exhibition of the work of St Dominic's Press, consisting mostly of woodcuts by Eric Gill. He and Pepler, the latter known as Douglas at this time, gave lectures later in the afternoon which were reported in the *Telegraph and Argus*, the local paper, under the large heading 'A CRITICISM OF BRADFORD'. Eric Gill told his audience that modern civilization was founded on the wrong things and that artists should reach an agreement as regards religion. Douglas Pepler was somewhat stronger in his criticism of Bradford. Taking paper mills as an example, he said that although huge mills had been built in the past century, the quality of the paper had not improved as the object was to make money rather than good paper. If civilization was based on Mammon, he recommended we should go back to what was meant by the worship of God. Although he had attempted to discover the point of view of Bradfordians, he concluded that, in his opinion, Bradford was the last place anyone would want to live. This was hardly likely to endear him to its manufacturers.

The worship of Mammon as represented by Gill's design for the proposed war memorial for Leeds University, *Christ's Expulsion of the Money-lenders from the Temple*, would cause a great controversy among that city's manufacturers some time hence, but this had not yet erupted when the three friends visited Leeds the following afternoon. Gill had a discussion about the proposed monument with Michael Sadler, the Vice-Chancellor of the university, before they went off to spend the day in Leeds. When they returned to the university, they discovered that they had gate-crashed a church reunion meeting which led to an 'amusing situation and conversation',[4] and it was not until after supper that they caught the train back to Bradford.

Monday was another busy day with more lectures for Gill and Pepler. In the morning Gill addressed the girls and mistresses of St Joseph's College on drawing; in the evening Pepler gave a lecture on education, at the Friends' Meeting House in Bradford. The afternoon had been taken up with further discussion on the Stations of the Cross and with reading.

The next day, as was usual when he was staying with Father O'Connor, Gill served the priest's daily Mass. After breakfast, the intrepid trio set off across the moors to Mountstead, the house at Ben Rhydding, where the Steinthal family were now living. This house was high above Ilkley and, in winter when there was snow on the ground, the master of the house used to ski down the moor to the station to catch the train to his business in Bradford. There was no snow on this fine March morning and Mrs Steinthal provided a welcome lunch of Yorkshire bacon, accompanied by wine, on their arrival. Eric found the daughter-in-law of the house, Maria Petrie, whom we last met drawing Father O'Connor's portrait under the table, to be a very charming person and quite a good sculptor. After supper back at St Cuthbert's there were further discussions about Father O'Connor's Stations. The following morning after a breakfast which featured an 1815 Marsala, not usually seen on a Yorkshire breakfast table, Gill and Pepler departed for Hawkesyard Priory.

At the beginning of 1921, Father O'Connor suggested to the writer and artist David Jones, that a visit to Eric Gill and the community living and working on Ditchling Common could be beneficial to him. They had probably come to know each through mutual contacts at the Westminster School of Art where Jones had enrolled after leaving the army. He had attended the Camberwell School of Art before enlisting in the Royal Welsh Fusiliers in 1915. Fighting with them in the trenches of the Western Front, he became seriously ill with trench fever and ended his soldiering in Ireland at the end of the First World War. Brought up as a Protestant, he had

nevertheless taken to calling in at the nearby Catholic cathedral
of Westminster to watch the sacrament of the Mass. He was
affected not only by the ritual and words of the Mass, but also
by the relationship between the sacrament and art. Much later,
when living in London in 1940, he began his long poem, *The
Kensington Mass*.

The Kensington of the title referred to the Carmelite church
in Kensington he attended, but the poem was dedicated to J.
O'C. and the first third describes the actions and sounds of his
language. His Irish roots are recalled with the Goidelic vowels
of his Celtic home county intermingled with the beauty of the
language he first heard and loved in Rome, or, to put it another
way, he spoke the Latin Mass with an Irish accent, for Father
O'Connor never lost either his Irish accent or his love of Latin.

The poem refers to 'Brigantia of the Fires sacred to half
Celtica as here in green Kildare'.[5] Coincidentally, Brigantia was
also a well-known figure in pagan Yorkshire, the West Riding
being the centre of the Celtic Brigantian kingdom. A homely
note is introduced as the writer describes how the priest's 'full
chin crumpled to the pectoral folds his newly washed focale'[6] as,
with hands above the altar, he calls for the help of the Blessed
departed. The poem appeared in *Agenda* in 1974 as an unfinished
draft of a poem David Jones was currently writing; it was hoped
that the full text would be published later but Jones became very
frail and died in the October. A version did appear, however, put
together from manuscripts by René Hague, who had married
Eric Gill's daughter, Joanna.

David Jones's wartime experiences had left him emotionally
scarred, questioning both his art and his religion, so at the
beginning of 1921 he decided to act on Father O'Connor's
advice to visit Eric Gill at Ditchling. A decision concerning his
religion was an early result of his visits and in September he
arrived on Father O'Connor's doorstep ready to be received
into the Catholic Church. A few days after his return to
Ditchling, Gill wrote to Father O'Connor expressing his delight
with David and hoping he would soon join them permanently,
which he did, with the encouragement of his headmaster at
Westminster, in November. He appears to have settled in

quickly for in December Gill told Father O'Connor that David would often read Shakespeare to Eric's daughter, Petra, as she sat sewing.

David was not the only young man in the community to be suffering the aftereffects of war, so he had something in common with the other young men he shared accommodation with, in the aptly named cottage The Sorrowful Mysteries. He learned wood and copper engraving, drew illustrations for books and assisted Gill with Father O'Connor's Stations, on which work was started in January 1921. Unlike the Westminster ones, these Stations were carved in their numerical order and in a letter written in February of that year,[7] Gill asked Father O'Connor if he thought *Jesus Is Condemned to Death* was a suitable title for the first Station. He also wanted Father O'Connor's suggestion for titles for the remainder, consisting of the same amount of letters as the first if possible, and asked if he would like inscribed texts on the backgrounds of the panels, as at Westminster, if there was enough space. Father O'Connor did like the idea so between them they worked out which texts to use, choosing texts in Latin for the Stations on the right-hand side of the church, and Greek texts for those on the left. Gill had stipulated that the Stations should start at the Sanctuary end of the epistle side, proceed down the church, and up the gospel side to finish at the Sanctuary.

Father O'Connor spent three days in April with Eric Gill at Ditchling and saw for himself how his Stations of the Cross were progressing. The low-relief engravings are on beer stone, smaller than the Westminster ones, with added colour. Father O'Connor considered this set of Stations to be more to Gill's own taste, as he was freer and more at ease as he worked. Parishioners recalled that when Gill was working on them in St Cuthbert's he was often seen in his carpet slippers, kneeling in prayer and reading his enormous Missal in his favourite spot, the top pew on the Lady Altar side.

Father O'Connor spent many happy hours at Ditchling and the fact that he was such an influence on Gill and the community showed him to be in sympathy with the ideas expressed so forcefully by Gill and Pepler on their recent visit

Station IV: *He Meets his Mother.*

Station XII: *He Dies*.

Station XIV: *He is Entombed*.

to Bradford. The idea of a guild, based on the worship of God rather than Mammon, had already been mooted, but it was only in September 1921 that the formation of the Guild of St Joseph and St Dominic was announced in *The Game*, a journal published by the Guild. The first requirement of members was to be a Dominican tertiary, though this was dropped in 1928, and work was held to be a form of divine worship. In accordance with the principles of Leo XIII's encyclical, *Rerum Novarum*, craftsmen must own their own workshops and tools. Father O'Connor wrote a review of Gill's *Last Essays*[8] and thought the small volume contained a lot of close reasoning and showed an intense loyalty to the papal encyclicals on Labour and Social Reform. As he had often been called upon to defend Gill's faith against those who had never read any of these earth-shaking documents, or if they had, had never retained anything of their content, he wrote with feeling.

Father O'Connor expressed his own views with regard to machines, arts and crafts in his little book of sermons, *A Month of Sundays*. He thought that if we had to live entirely with machine-made articles, we should go mad, in fact we were going mad, this being due in a large part to the lack of craftsmen and craftsmanship and a number of bad artists attempting to make a mystery of art. 'Artists and craftsmen should be one in everything', he wrote, 'since Fine Art is to Applied Art or Craftsmanship what singing is to speaking: what dancing is to walking.' He continued, 'Snobbery separated Fine Art from Craft, and humility must join them up again.'[9]

Study of *Rerum Novarum* had inspired Hilaire Belloc to express his thoughts on Distributism, an alternative to Capitalism and Socialism, in his book, *The Servile State,* first published in 1912. The Distributist League was founded in 1926 and in 1936 Belloc wrote *An Essay on the Restoration of Property,* in which he suggested how a distributive society might look and how it could be achieved. Chesterton contributed to the movement by financing and editing *G. K.'s Weekly*, a journal promoting Distributism which Chesterton revived from *New Witness,* owned by his brother and which Gilbert had edited while Cecil was away fighting and, dying, during the First World War. This, in turn, had evolved from *The Eye-Witness,* founded by Belloc in 1911.

The Central Branch of The Distributist League held their meetings at The Devereux public house off the Strand in London, while there were other large branches in Birmingham, Liverpool and Glasgow. A Bradford branch was mooted at the beginning of 1927 and came into being in May with a talk by the branch secretary, Mrs Margaret Healey, who explained the objects and works of the League.

The early meetings were held in St Patrick's schoolrooms but, after the discussion following a paper on the history of guilds had to be curtailed owing to the premises closing, it was decided that future meetings should be held at St Cuthbert's Parochial Hall on Wilmer Road. Apart from the occasional meeting at the Mikado Café in Godwin Street, Church House on North Parade, or the home of the secretary, they continued to be held there until the demise of the branch.

In December 1927, the branch members discussed ways and means of effectively spreading Distributism in Bradford, agreeing example as well as precept should be given when possible. It was also agreed that the encouragement of smallholdings should form an essential part of Distributist propaganda. Co-partnership as a step between present capitalism and a future Distributist State, was discussed in early April 1928 but it was pointed out that this would be useless unless adopted by other branches.

The meeting on 28 April ended in unanimous agreement that the establishment of a Distributist State and the moulding of the large northern industries by encouraging individual workers to set up as craftsmen was the work of centuries. In order to bring about the de-centralization of industry, a scheme of real co-partnership needed to be worked out which would apply to present-day industries. Only through co-partnership could workers be educated and encouraged to set up as independent individuals or in small groups. It was hoped that this scheme, along with the transformation of Trade Unions to Guilds, and all the other League principles regarding land and so on, would bring about a Distributist State as quickly as humanly possible. Accordingly, the Branch intended to work out Co-partnership proposals to submit to the League and especially to the northern branches. High ideals no doubt, but in practice things did not go according to plan.

A discussion followed a talk entitled *Liberty and Property* by Mr F. Alderson in November, and plans were afoot for a series of propaganda meetings to be held in the city. The following month, however, the unpleasant fact had to faced that no proper meetings could be held due to lack of efficient speakers, not to mention the lack of a practical policy likely to appeal to the thousands of textile workers who, like themselves, earned their living in the capitalist mills of Bradford.

In the 1929 General Election, members of the Bradford branch of the Distributist League were being urged to vote for the party likely to get the least number of votes in order to prevent one party getting an overwhelming majority. It was judged better that the three parties should be required to bargain rather than one party having the power to dictate, thus enabling them to further restrict liberties without encountering opposition. The Distributists were no doubt happy with the outcome of the election which resulted in the large majority held by the Conservatives since 1924 being overturned, and a win for the Labour Party, but without an overall majority which left the Liberal Party holding the balance of power.

Labour won all three seats in Bradford, with two Conservatives losing their seats, one of them Father O'Connor's friend Anthony Gadie. The third seat was regained from the Liberal member by Fred Jowett who, in 1904, had instigated the provision of free school meals, making Bradford the first council to do so. It seems the local Distributists, if they had voted as suggested, had not been able to affect the local results.

The meeting held at St Cuthbert's Parochial Hall in November, discussed an idea (not recorded) to arouse interest in the League which was to be passed on to the League Secretary. Suggestions were also made for the manifesto, without much hope it seems as in *G. K.'s Weekly* the following spring, several members around the country pointed out that the prime defect of the Distributist Manifesto was that it had not yet appeared!

The Bradford Branch seems to have kept a low profile for

the next couple of years, though no doubt meetings were being held if not reported. The First Summer Conference of the Distributist League was held over three days at Douai School in September 1931 but was attended by only twenty-five members. A lack of funds saw urgent appeals being made to members in December.

How many of Father O'Connor's parishioners were members of the League is not known due to the lack of records, but one of them, Mr Leo Pollack, gave a paper on Co-operative Banking to the branch meeting in March 1933. Animated discussions followed a speech on Co-Partnership by E. Wilson in May and 'Why Distributists should not support Co-Partnership' by M. White in June. F. Alderson gave two papers concerning Distributists and Fascists in 1933 and 1934.

The last entry for the Bradford Branch appears in *G. K.'s Weekly* on 5 April 1934 when M. White spoke on 'Guilds in the Middle Ages'. As these infrequent notes in the League branches' column of the journal are the only records of the Bradford Distributists which have come to light, it is impossible to say when they finally disbanded. Though the meetings were taking place in St Cuthbert's church hall, Father O'Connor himself is silent on the subject, as are local newspapers and although many branches began to re-form after the war, Bradford does not seem to have been one of them.

In July 1921, Desmond Chute accompanied Eric Gill on his next visit to Bradford. They were met by Charles Rutherston, with whom Chute was to stay, but they all had supper together at the presbytery. Next day Father O'Connor and Gill walked to Rutherston's 'forbidding stone mansion',[10] as his nephew John Rothenstein described it, in an area of Heaton occupied mainly by mill owners or professional people. The visitors had come to view Rutherston's impressive art collection, one of the most important collections of modern English work in the country, comprising paintings, drawings and sculpture, together with ancient oriental pottery, bronzes and jade. Father O'Connor was not one to be overawed by such a collection, as he himself collected similar treasures, though on a slightly more modest scale.

Though Charles Rutherston had been a very successful partner in his father's firm, he was not a hard-headed capitalist but the possessor of a social conscience who sought out ways of benefiting others. He could be said to practise his own brand of Distributism, not least by donating, anonymously, £12,000 towards redemption of the country's National Debt after the First World War. He believed that art was one of life's necessities rather than a luxury and that as a collector of works of art he should not selfishly keep them to himself. He considered his role to be rather that of a trustee and as such he devised a plan to put his collection to practical service.

Rutherston constantly loaned works of art to galleries, museums, exhibitions and educational institutes and he planned to donate the collection to a gallery with the proviso that the works of art should continue to be circulated. He offered it to the Cartwright Hall Art Gallery in Bradford, but knowing the opposition faced by his brother, William Rothenstein, and the committee of London artists when they tried to introduce some of the best contemporary art into the Gallery's opening exhibition in 1904, he was not surprised when it was refused. Manchester City Art Gallery were more than pleased to accept it and carried out his wishes, circulating the art to galleries and schools in both Lancashire and Yorkshire, even to Bradford!

The object of Eric Gill's and Desmond Chute's visit to Bradford was to work on the Stations but they managed to fit in another social engagement, this one in Dewsbury where they attended the consecration of the Church of Our Lady and St Paulinus. After lunch with the bishop and local clergy, they went on to Heckmondwike where they had tea with Father O'Connor's successor at the Church of the Holy Spirit. In the evening, back at St Cuthbert's, Eric made his confession to Father O'Connor and after supper talked over what he termed his 'affairs'[11] regarding his daughter Elizabeth. Father O'Connor was Eric Gill's friend as well as confessor, and, though Eric frequently went to confession, there were times when only Father O'Connor would do, and this was perhaps one of them. Gill's somewhat unusual attitude to sexual matters is now well known, his incestuous relations with his sisters, his sexual experiments with his daughters, his naked cavorting with house guests such as Moira Gibbings, with the full knowledge and approval of her husband, Robert. Gill is quite explicit in his *Diaries* about in what he and his daughters indulged, which was more in the nature of satisfying his curiosity rather than his passion. His daughters seem to have accepted this behaviour as part of their altogether uncommon upbringing and appear not to have been left feeling abused as they went on to have happy marriages. Others though continue to be offended and in the late 1990s Cardinal Basil Hume was asked to remove Gill's Stations of the Cross from Westminster Cathedral by a group of victims of sexual abuse. While sympathetic to such victims, the request was refused as the carvings were considered to be beautiful works of art, while their artistic value was unconnected to the morals of the artist.

Father O'Connor gave his personal impression of Gill as artist in an article he wrote for *The Bookman* in 1930.[12] Gill was constantly trying to see into things, as for instance he would mentally unclothe a newspaper photograph of a clothed figure in action in order to produce a realistic study of a nude. Late one evening, Father O'Connor made the assertion that a Madonna and Child inside a vesica would be sublime. Unfortunately Gill, as was his way, questioned why this should be so, leaving the priest unable to go to bed until he had given both a definition of sublime and the reasons why it would be. This was not wasted as Eric took up the suggestion and the wood engraving, *Madonna and Child in vesica* duly appeared in 1929.

Gill's constant desire to know why something should be so was, according to his *Diaries*, often the reason for his visits to his daughters' bedroom, but he also wrote that the visits must stop, which showed him to be struggling with his conscience and not feeling entirely free from guilt. He knew Father O'Connor understood him, saw into the workings of his mind, 'knew where he was coming from' in today's parlance, no doubt making it easier for Gill to confess his sins to him. Father O'Connor was not only Gill's friend but a friend to all the family who would not have stood by and done nothing if any of them had shown signs of distress and while Gill's actions were certainly unusual, they were not those of a paedophile.

In time, Father O'Connor evolved his own apology for Gill's behaviour and told both Gill himself and David Jones that those who led only a sheltered life were in no position to condemn the nude in art. Sexual abnormality was much more difficult to cope with than vulgar behaviour and anything that kept sexual attraction normal was not to be condemned. Father O'Connor recalled being told many years ago by a Redemptorist Father that it was the uneducated girls who worked in the mills who saw and said everything they had a mind to, who were much more to be trusted out alone than those whose innocence was founded on ignorance. Nothing had ever occurred to make him doubt the truth of this. His faith in Eric Gill was accounted for by just such reason.

Gill's discussion with Father O'Connor after supper concerning his daughter Elizabeth resulted in her being sent to Gruyères in Switzerland only a couple of months later. Ostensibly she went to a small hotel to learn to cook and make cheese, and to distract her from the attention of Pepler' s son. Gill disapproved of this on the grounds of their youth, but it also removed temptation from her father, as Father O'Connor no doubt pointed out. After returning home, Eric wrote to thank him for all the kindness, both spiritual and material, he had shown. Desmond Chute accompanied Gill and Elizabeth to Gruyères before continuing to Fribourg where he was to study for the priesthood.

Before Gill and Chute completed their visit to Bradford in July 1921, there was another meeting in Leeds with Michael Sadler to discuss the war memorial, an invitation to dinner with Father Daly at St Anne's in Keighley and tea with the Pollack family, wealthy parishioners of St Cuthbert's. A further visit to the home of Charles Rutherston, proved to be a profitable evening for Eric Gill when he was introduced to a wealthy neighbour, Asa Lingard. Lingard's father had opened a department store in Bradford in 1875 and when he died, in 1903, he was succeeded by his son. Asa took little active interest in the prosperous business he had inherited but became a well-respected art expert, acquiring a fine collection of paintings and sculpture, books, furniture, and early Chinese porcelain. He already possessed a sculpture by Gill, *Torso* in Bath stone, but Eric was able to sell him that evening *Mother and Child* and *Andiómené*, another sculpture in Bath stone.

Gill's last task before leaving was to write a letter entitled 'The Secret of Art' to a local newspaper, the *Yorkshire Observer,* which he delivered by hand. This was in reply to a report of a lecture on Art given by Michael Sadler in Keighley, in which he voices the opinions of modern critics but fails to draw any conclusion from them. Gill thought that by so doing he had omitted the most important part of the lecture and proceeded to rectify the omission.

The beginning of February 1922 saw completion of the fourth Station of the Cross, entitled *He Meets His Mother*, except for the colouring. Gill thought the figure of Our Lady looked particularly well, thanks to Desmond Chute's drawing. During the carving of the Station, however, Gill had altered it slightly causing the soldier to thrust a nail towards Our Lady. He sent a photograph for Chute to compare with his drawing, explaining that what he had lost in facial expression, he had tried to gain in expressive attitude.

Eric Gill's first reference to *Art et Scholastique,* the recently published book by the French philosopher Jacques Maritain, appeared in his diary entry for 23 April 1922, when both he and Pepler were reading it. The Frenchman Jacques Maritain and his Russian-Jewish wife converted to Catholicism in 1906, two years after their marriage. A professor of modern philosophy, he began an intensive study of the writings of St Thomas Aquinas and came to be regarded as the leading lay exponent of Thomism. Published in 1920, *Art et Scholastique* was just becoming known in England when Gill first read it, but was destined to have a profound effect on the community at Ditchling, coming to dominate Gill's own ideas on Art in relation to Prudence and Christianity.

Father O'Connor had been in Ditchling in March but when he was there again at the end of April he found himself giving an oral translation of Maritain's book. When it was decided that an English translation should be one of the first books to be printed and published at Ditchling, it was Father O'Connor who was called upon to undertake the task and the translation began in earnest next day. Gill, meanwhile, was carving *The Divine Lovers,* a pair of haloed, hugging figures in boxwood, and wielding the dictionary. One of Gill's remarkable qualities was this ability of being able to conduct a difficult conversation while continuing to work with his hands.

The translation was interrupted when Father O'Connor left for Rome at the beginning of May. On his way home, he met up with the Gills in Switzerland where they had gone to visit Elizabeth. Father O'Connor was once again called upon to read Maritain's book aloud, on this occasion under the trees and to the sound of cowbells. They all stayed a few days at the hotel where Elizabeth was working and while Father O'Connor settled down to some serious translating, Eric returned to his *Divine Lovers.* On 30 May, they took the train to Fribourg to the Albertinum, where Desmond Chute was studying for the priesthood. The following morning, after saying Mass at the Albertinum, Father O'Connor left for England and the Gills took their daughter back to Gruyère. Elizabeth came home for good at the beginning of October.

Later that month Father O'Connor wrote to Gill with news of a recent acquisition, a painting by Watteau for which he had paid the sum of twenty-three shillings. Gill replied that as this was probably the amount the artist himself had been paid, he rejoiced that Father O'Connor had the satisfaction of having done the dealers and not for the first time.

Father O'Connor continued the translation of *Art and Scholastique* when back at St Cuthbert's. There was a suggestion that the translation should first appear in serial form in *The Game,* but Father O'Connor advised against this and it was agreed that it would come out in book form. During the publication of the book by St Dominic's Press, the community would first attend sung Office in the chapel, and spend the rest of the morning discussing the finer points of Maritain's philosophy. The book was in the final proof stage by the end of May 1923 and came out later that year under the title *The Philosophy of Art,* with an introduction by Eric Gill. The book was considered by some to be not as entirely accurate in the translation of the precise Thomistic terms as was the second translation, by J. F. Scanlan published in 1930, but Eric Gill found its rich humanity and humour unsurpassable. He thought it a merciful and blessed dispensation on the part of divine providence that such a precious book should have had its first English translation published by the beautiful, if somewhat inexperienced, Ditchling press. When Gill had lunch with Maritain in Paris, he told Father O'Connor that he wished he had been there as Maritain spoke no English. Fortunately Hilary Pepler had understood what was said and, aided by Elizabeth Gill, they had managed to hold a conversation.

On 14 May 1923, Eric Gill and his apprentice stone-carver, Joseph Cribb, arrived at St Cuthbert's for a four-night stay. The latter was another young man who sought refuge from the trenches of the First World War and had found it at Ditchling in 1921. He had come north to assist Gill in the final work on the Leeds war memorial which was due to be finished and in place by June. They travelled each day to Leeds to work on it and finished the job on a very wet, snowy, and generally horrible day, but they had, as usual, an enjoyable visit with Father O'Connor. Gill spent any spare moments writing the lecture he was to give to the London University Catholic Students' Club at the end of the week and where he went directly from Bradford. He later wrote to thank Father O'Connor for his hospitality, adding that he had come away with several valuable pearls of wisdom probably after he had once more unburdened his soul to the priest both in and out of the confessional.

The controversy concerning the Leeds war memorial was now beginning with much discussion on the subject in the local papers. Gill had himself been interviewed by a national newspaper but asked Father O'Connor to send him cuttings from the Yorkshire papers, of which there were plenty. Along the cornice of the memorial was a Latin inscription from St James's Epistle, translated as 'Go now, you rich men, weep and howl in your miseries which shall come upon you.'[13] As the figures in the panel were in modern dress, representing the fashionable folk of Leeds, politicians, financiers, even a pawnbroker and his clerk, the monument was bound to cause comment. Once this major work was out of the way, Gill could return to work on the Bradford Stations of the Cross, which he hoped to complete the following year.

When Father O'Connor was not translating French philosophy, he was busy writing the words for a children's Mass which was set to music by Dom Alphege Shebbeare, OSB. This was sung at St Benedict's, at Hindley in Lancashire, and published in 1923 as *The Hindley Children's Mass*. He later wrote to his friend, Dame Werburg Welch, that in Scotland a monsignor had found the work too classical but in Lancashire the children sang it in the street. Father O'Connor may have referred to himself as an old hymn-tinker but the critic who reviewed the piece in *Catholic Book Notes* thought the words were 'worthy of the poet who composed them'.

Father O'Connor was the inspiration, if somewhat indirectly, behind another young man who became a Distributist and eventually a member of the Guild of St Joseph and St Dominic working on Ditchling Common. The KilBride family were both St Cuthbert parishioners and great friends of the priest. John Valentine Dennis KilBride, the only son of the family, was born in 1897, and educated at St Bede's Grammar School. Val, as he was always known, began an apprenticeship at George Armitage Ltd, a dyeing firm founded by his maternal great-grandfather, but this was interrupted by the First World War. Demobilized in 1919 at the age of twenty-two, he resumed his apprenticeship and studies at the Bradford Technical College. Just before the outbreak of war, most of the dyers in Bradford had combined to become the Bradford Dyers' Association and Val was dismayed to discover that specialization had been introduced and Armitages were now only black dyers, the colour dyeing being done elsewhere. To add to his disappointment this whole process was mechanized, while his heart was set on being a craftsman.

Father O'Connor had introduced Val to the writings of Belloc and Chesterton and the cause of Distributism and soon he was reading widely on the subject in books and *New Witness*. Val's son, Gilbert, himself a silk weaver and vestment maker in Wales, sent me a copy of his father's unpublished

memoirs in which he explained the great influence Belloc and
Chesterton had on Catholic young people in the 1920s. They
gave them confidence and a self-respect that carried them on to
many ventures. Unlike their fathers who had an inferiority
complex about their religion and generally lived together in
ghettos, these young people considered themselves the
avant-garde and were immensely proud of being Catholics.
Their common faith drew them together only for action and one
of their actions was the following of Belloc's Distributism.

Val KilBride came to the conclusion that a peasantry and an
industry of craftsmen were the answer to the social problems of
the time, so, having finished his apprenticeship to industrial
dyeing, he decided that it was a craftsman he would become.
He chose to become a weaver, an obvious choice perhaps in a
woollen city such as Bradford, but the evening textile courses
he had attended at Bradford Technical College were concerned
with mechanized trade. It was his sister who told him that
Father O'Connor knew some Catholic workmen who were
building their own houses and workshops on Ditchling
Common. One of his two sisters, Josephine, taught at St
Cuthbert's Primary School, and both his sisters were in a choir
which Father O'Connor was training to sing plainchant, having
fallen out with the operatic choir in his church!

It was not to Ditchling that Val went first however, but
across the Pennines to Lancashire to the Guild of St Margaret
of Scotland. Lack of finance caused the failure of this project
and when Father O'Connor heard about this he was determined
that Val should join the community at Ditchling. Val was
familiar with the work of the weaver Ethel Mairet, having seen
examples in a Design and Industry exhibition at the Bradford
Art Gallery. He had also read and been impressed with her
book on Vegetable Dyes. He had been introduced to her at an
exhibition in Lancashire and now contacted her again, resulting
in his becoming her pupil and lodging in her house in Ditchling
village. Father O'Connor introduced Val to his friends on the
Common and he was soon visiting them. In 1925, after
eighteen months with Ethel Mairet, he moved into Eric's old
workshop on the Common, as Gill had by then had moved to

Capel-y-ffyn, and the following year, after becoming a Tertiary, he joined the Guild of St Joseph and St Dominic.

Val KilBride, together with his eventual partner Bernard Brocklehurst, specialized in the making of silk vestments, reviving the gothic draped style of chasuble woven from a single piece of material without seams. Val carried out commissions on both sides of the Atlantic, notably in America for the Washington Catholic Cathedral, and went on to win the Gold Medal of the Catholic Arts Association for his contribution to ecclesiastical art. His daughter Jenny continued the family tradition of weaving and dyeing in Ditchling and was the first woman member of the Guild, while his grandson, Ewan Clayton a calligrapher, was the last member to join in 1982.

Gill had been rushing to get the St Cuthbert's Stations of the Cross finished for Good Friday, 1924 but as Father O'Connor had been able to arrange a visit to Ditchling at Easter he had a little breathing space. He was especially relieved as he had to re-cut the title on Station VIII when the priest changed his mind about the one he had chosen originally.

On the first evening of his visit there were songs after supper at Hopkins Crank, Father O'Connor probably providing some of the entertainment himself. He had a more important part in a small ceremony a few days later. David Jones was now settled at Ditchling, to the extent of falling in love with Petra Gill, Eric's second daughter. After some discussion, her parents agreed to their engagement although, at twenty-eight, David was ten years older than their daughter. The Guild members assembled to witness their betrothal before Father O'Connor, who later wrote out the terms of the engagement. But it was not to last and Petra eventually married while David remained a bachelor all his life.

The Stations of the Cross were eventually packed and despatched to Bradford on 21 and 22 May to be followed by Eric Gill and David Jones in early June to finish and colour them. Desmond Chute had completed a number of designs for the Stations, the fourteenth, *He is Entombed*, is based on William Blake's tempera painting *The Body of Christ Borne to the Tomb*. Though Gill thought them very admirable and that

Chute had a gift for that kind of illustration, he had not always used them. He fancied his own gift was more physical, more objective and sensual.

Their visit to Bradford was not all work for Gill and Jones, as usual there were a number of social engagements to fit in. Together with Father O'Connor they visited Leeds to see the university war memorial and have tea with the Newman Society. In Bradford they fitted in a visit to Val KilBride's mother, updating her on her son's progress working with Ethel Mairet. They paid a couple of visits to the Cartwright Hall Art Gallery, one with Father O'Connor who introduced them to the curator. Work on the Stations was finally completed on17 June, and after supper and confession, the talk again concerned Eric's affairs, not of the sexual kind in this instance but rather financial. The next day, he and David were going straight to London to meet Father Vincent McNabb at St Dominic's Priory for a meeting with Hilary Pepler and carpenter, loom-maker, and Guild member, George Maxwell, to discuss matters concerning the Guild. The following month Gill resigned from the Guild and in August he moved to Capel-y-ffin, Wales.

Father O'Connor's next literary collaboration with Eric Gill caused something of an outcry in certain religious circles. Robert Gibbings, who had acquired the Golden Cockerel Press in 1924, commissioned Gill to do the engravings for *The Song of Songs*. Not wishing to offend the Catholic Church in any way, Gill insisted on using text from the Douay version of the Bible but when Gibbings, himself an agnostic, had difficulty setting it up, Gill referred him to Father O'Connor. After some demur, the latter took on the editing and had plenty of his own ideas on the subject. The Preface calls the edition 'a version of versions of the work',[14] rather than a fresh translation.

Eric's first visit to Bradford after his move to Wales was at the end of January and beginning of February 1925. He was occupied finishing some drawings but found time to join Father O'Connor for dinner with Father Daly at St Anne's in Keighley where they met Frank Mullins, a Wagnerian tenor with the British National Opera Company. Gill accompanied Charles Rutherston on a visit to his parents' graves and went on with him to the art school in Bradford. Charles's nephew, John Rothenstein, called in at the presbytery a couple of times after supper, on the second occasion as Eric was writing to John's father, William. After much consideration he was turning down William's offer of an appointment as visiting professor in wood-engraving and stone-carving at the Royal College of Art, mainly as he wasn't in accord with Williams's aims for the future for the college. From Bradford, Gill went straight to visit Robert Gibbings and the following September Father O'Connor went to Birmingham to join them both for a discussion on the final proofs of *The Song of Songs*. Just a few days later Gibbings started printing the limited edition of seven hundred and fifty, thirty of which were hand-coloured. Gill had made eighteen wood engravings for the illustrations, but thought eighteen was really rather too many for the text.

Eric was very grateful for Desmond Chute's appreciation and for the, mostly, enthusiastic approval of the book as this was not how it was generally received by the clergy. *The Song of Songs* is from the Old Testament *Book of Solomon* whose poems are now generally interpreted as originally being love songs, probably intended for use at Jewish weddings and exalting conjugal love. It was Eric Gill's somewhat explicit engravings of conjugal love between Christ and the female figure of his bride, representing his Church, that gave cause for concern in certain quarters. One priest labelled it immoral, saying it ought not to have been published and was a disgrace to Gill's name. In reply to Father Bede Jarrett,[15] who shrank from Gill's realistic acceptance of the flesh and wished to have the book suppressed, Gill said his best defence was to name his authority, which he did not want to do as he was willing to take any blame himself. Certain priests had approved the work, however, and he had not acted without the approval of at least one competent and responsible Catholic priest. As Father O'Connor was not credited in the book itself, his own contribution was not a matter of general knowledge. Gill's American admirers were not able to judge its qualities for themselves as US Custom officials deemed the book unfit to be seen in their country.

Havelock Ellis, the English author of many books on the

psychology of sex, suggested that Ernest Renan's translation of
The Song of Songs, published in 1860, so closely resembled
Gill's edition that he must have known of it. Gill wrote to
Father O'Connor[16] to see if he was indeed acquainted with it,
if he wasn't he could lend him a second-hand copy he had
bought recently which, incidentally, had come from a Bradford
bookshop. His next letter[17] thanked Father O'Connor for his
reply and said he would pass the information on to the proper
quarter, unfortunately he didn't say what that information was.
There is no mention of a book by Renan in the sale catalogue
of his books compiled on Father O'Connor's death, but an
earlier, 1803, American translation of *Song of Songs* appears
on a handwritten list.

Father O'Connor's next collaboration with Eric Gill, *The
Song of the Soul,* received much less attention, though the wood
engravings were as explicit as those in *The Song of Songs.* The
book, published by at Capel-y-ffin in 1927 in a limited edition of
150, was translated by Father O'Connor from *Canciones entre el
alma y Christo su esposo* by the poet and mystic, St John of the
Cross, who first started writing the work in a Toledo prison cell
but later revised and completed it. From his introduction to the
book, we can see that this was not the only work by St John of
the Cross with which Father O'Connor was familiar. Study of
these had helped his understanding of how poets look into things
rather than around them, similarly how mystics seeing God and
his creatures unveiled allows them to behold their very essence.
Lacking this poetic or mystic insight deprives lesser mortals the
ability to perceive the essence of anything, leaving us merely to
deduce that essence from qualities revealed to our senses.
Perhaps it was this knowledge that enabled Father O'Connor to
understand that Eric Gill, though he was in no way comparing
him to a mystic, as a sculptor did see rather more than some.

When Desmond Chute was ordained later the same year, 25
September 1927, at Downside Abbey, Father O'Connor
attended the ceremony but Eric Gill was unable to do so. He
expressed his regret at being unable to attend the 'wedding', his
belief that the Church was the bride of Christ still being very
much at the forefront of his mind at this time.

In February 1928, Eric Gill was to lecture to the Catholic University Students in Manchester on Art and Prudence and took the opportunity of the visit north to spend the weekend with Father O'Connor. As Art and Prudence was a topic covered by Jacques Maritain in *Art et Scholastique,* there was sure to be further discussion on the subject, but in between writing the lecture Gill, as usual on these visits, found time for socializing. This weekend included lunch at an Oyster Bar, an Old Boys' Dinner at St Bede's Grammar School and a visit to the opera to see *Aida.* They also took a walk to see the war memorial at St Bede's designed and carved by their friend Joseph Cribb, which had been unveiled in September 1926.

After only four years or so, in October 1928, the Gill family were on the move again, this time to a farmhouse and outbuildings known collectively as Pigotts, near High Wycombe in Buckinghamshire. Eric wrote to Father O'Connor the following month setting out his plans for the proposed chapel at Pigotts. He replied[18] that the bishop, Dudley Cary-Elwes, would not approve of Gill's plans and, though there was no rule against his ideas, Father O'Connor advised him to tread warily. Typically, however, he also told him to go ahead and do it anyway, seeking approval later. He added a few suggestions of his own and remarked that although some priests tended to become flustered on the altar and did not take kindly to new ideas, he himself would be very happy to say Mass there.

The chapel was not ready for use until the following year, about the same time as a telephone was installed at Pigotts. Gill's first use of the instrument was to summons the Chestertons and Father O'Connor to the blessing of the chapel. They all duly arrived the next day and on 7 June 1929 Father O'Connor, with Eric serving, celebrated the first Mass held in the chapel. The visit was commemorated by Gill drawing a portrait of Father O'Connor.

In March of the year same, Father O'Connor had written a review in *Blackfriars* of *The Mysteriousness of Marriage* by Jeremy Taylor, with illustrations by Denis Tegetmeier. While he was not very impressed with the sermons which made up the text, he was very impressed by the six engravings of

Joseph Cribb's war memorial, St Bede's Grammar School.

Tegetmeier. It seemed to Father O'Connor that a new star had arisen and he looked forward to even greater success for his very original work. Tegetmeier was another First World War victim who shared lodgings with David Jones at Ditchling. It was in order to marry Denis that Petra Gill broke off her engagement to David, but when the ceremony took place in January 1930, David was one of the two witnesses and they all remained friends.

The end of the decade brought promotion for Father O'Connor to the position of The Very Reverend Dean of North Bradford.

Notes

1. Gill, *Autobiography*, p. 205.
2. Ibid., p. 206.
3. Ibid., p. 210.
4. Gill, *Diary*, 7 March 1920.
5. Jones, 'Kensington Mass', *Agenda*, p. 6.
6. Ibid.
7. Gill, *Letter*, 7 February 1921.
8. O'Connor, 'Review of Gill's *Last Essays*', pp. 56–8.
9. O'Connor, *Month of Sundays*, p.159.
10. Rothenstein, J. *Summer's Lease*.
11. Gill, *Diary*, 25 July 1921.
12. O'Connor, *Eric Gill: The Searcher for Reality*, p. 190.
13. Speaight, *The Life of Eric Gill*, p. 128..
14. Preface, *The Song of Songs*.
15. Speaight, *The Life of Eric Gill*, p. 175.
16. Gill, *Letter*, 15 November 1926.
17. Gill, *Letter*, 23 December 1926.
18. O'Connor, *Letter*, 9 December 1928, Tate Gallery.

Chapter 8

1912–26: The Chestertons Convert to Catholicism

The news that Gilbert Keith Chesterton had converted to Catholicism in 1922 sent shock waves around the world, but GK had first broached the subject to Father O'Connor on a train to Ilkley in 1912. They were returning from Leeds, where they had been taking part in the discussion at the Ladies' Debating Society previously referred to in chapter four, when GK told Father O'Connor that he had made up his mind to be received into the Catholic Church. This was thrilling news but hardly surprising to the priest who had long felt that GK had a natural affinity to Catholicism, but, it being a principle with Father O'Connor to strengthen what faith a man had rather than weaken it, he had never attacked Chesterton's Anglicanism. GK admitted that now the only reason he was holding back was that he was waiting for Frances to come with him. Father O'Connor understood perfectly, once remarking to Josephine Ward, whose daughter Maisie was Chesterton's biographer, that Gilbert would need Frances to take him to church, find his place in his prayer book, and examine his conscience for him when he went to confession. Gilbert continued to wait for some years but it was a step that eventually he did have to take alone as Frances continued her struggle for a further four years before making the final decision to follow her husband into the Catholic Church.

Two years passed after the talk on the train before the matter was raised again, this time in more dire circumstances. On 16

October 1914, Frances wrote to Father O'Connor expressing her anxiety about her husband who was 'appallingly busy',[1] writing a series of pamphlets for the Government and keeping *New Witness* going while brother Cecil was in the trenches. By the end of November Frances was asking for Father O'Connor's prayers on behalf of Gilbert who was now seriously ill but who continued to read a lot and dictate a little. A relapse followed on Christmas Eve, now Gilbert was desperately ill, often unconscious and very weak with what Father O'Connor described as 'gout all over'[2] as his brain, stomach and lungs were affected. Frances was in a state of despair and thought it was likely her husband would ask for his friend, in which case she would telegraph him.

A few days later, Father O'Connor received a letter from Josephine (Mrs Wilfrid) Ward,[3] who at the time he had not met but, as she had heard him often spoken about by their mutual friends the Chestertons, she had decided to write to him. Believing Gilbert to have considered becoming a Catholic, she wanted Father O'Connor to know how ill he was in case the priest thought it expedient to hasten to his bedside to give Gilbert the opportunity to speak to him on the matter. In a postscript, she added that she wished to keep their correspondence private as she thought it might cause harm if she was thought to be interfering.

On receiving confirmation that he would indeed attempt to see Gilbert, Mrs Ward suggested that, in order to make the mission less obvious, Father O'Connor take a short holiday in London so it would not be considered unusual if he just happened to slip down to Beaconsfield! Off Father O'Connor went to meet Mrs Ward at the Ladies' Club in London, before going on to Beaconsfield the same afternoon. He was prepared to give Gilbert the Last Rites on the strength of Gilbert's remarks on the Ilkley train, but, when Father O'Connor arrived at the house, Frances explained that her husband was now so seriously ill that only she was allowed to see him, and that when he was asleep. When he explained why he had wanted to see GK, Frances remarked 'So that is what Gilbert meant by all the dark hints about being buried in Kensal Green, and so on. I never could make head or tail. I suppose he wanted to put it to me straightforwardly, but couldn't bring himself to the crisis.'[4] St Mary's Roman Catholic Cemetery at Kensal Green is the lasting resting place of many Catholics, among them a number of celebrities, but unfortunately Frances hadn't been able to make the connection at which her husband had hinted. She thought it was just the sort of thing though that he would do. Josephine Ward hoped Father O'Connor's talk with Frances would have done her good, and that Frances was nearer the Church than she herself knew. Meanwhile they would have to continue to hope and pray for them both.

Gilbert needed his wife at his side and was reluctant to take such an important step as conversion to Catholicism without taking her with him, but Frances was not yet ready to commit herself. It was a troubling situation for them both but, when Gilbert began to show signs of recovery later in the month, she hoped and prayed he would soon be fit enough to say what he wanted to do. It made her dreadfully unhappy not knowing what he would like her to do if and when he was so critically ill in the future. His parents, she was sure, would never forgive her if she acted only on her own authority. Her great hope was that God would restore Gilbert to health enough in order for him to make this momentous decision and inform her of his wishes, even if death was to follow. As Gilbert did grow stronger physically and mentally, she hoped it would not be long before the subject could be raised.

Gilbert's health continued to improve, but only slowly, throughout the rest of January and February and in March he asked his wife if she had thought he was going to die, which she admitted she had at times. On the eve of Easter, 1915, although Gilbert's mind was beginning to clear, he still found it difficult to distinguish between the real and unreal. He asked Frances if Father O'Connor had known how ill he had been and, on hearing that she often wrote to him, Gilbert said that he would like to see him soon as he wanted a talk with him. During Gilbert's illness, Father O'Connor noted that many Catholics prayed for him, persuading the priest that they already felt that in some mysterious way Gilbert was already a member of their Church and recognized his claim to the support their prayers offered.

On a visit to Beaconsfield a few days after Easter, Father O'Connor was pleased to note that, although Gilbert's clothes now fitted only where they touched, he did look fifteen years younger. Restored to health, Gilbert was still not ready to face head-on the problem which had so greatly troubled Frances during his illness, and to which Gilbert had hinted. The subject of one, or both of them, converting to Catholicism was never raised by Gilbert or Frances during Father O'Connor's visit so he too remained silent on the subject, in fact another five years passed before the subject was once more discussed.

Letters from Beaconsfield in Chesterton's own hand were rare but Father O'Connor received one at Christmas 1920.[5] 'The confused scrawl', as the writer himself put it, brought the news of the Chestertons forthcoming trip to America. Freed from the demands of his work on the *New Witness*, he hoped to have a proper talk with his wife, after which he would like to discuss important matters, 'the most important things there are', with the priest. He would then like to consult his Anglo-Catholic friends, but he felt this would be a farewell. It wasn't, though the month in America had given them some breathing space. Gilbert's excuses about pressure of work and the delicate health of Frances were not really the main reason that he still fought shy of taking the step which he longed to take. Father O'Connor, like Frances, knew the real reason was 'his congenital aversion to starting a crisis'.[6]

It was some eighteen months later, on 11 July 1922, that Chesterton wrote the letter for which Father O'Connor had been waiting patiently for the past ten years. He sent, as ever, in great haste, an urgent plea for help to resolve the many things troubling him, especially the most serious religious ones. Feeling he could no longer make excuses, and Father O'Connor being the person that both he and Frances thought of with most affection, of all who could help in the matter, Gilbert wished him to visit them as soon as the following week if possible. Father O'Connor assured him that he was at their disposal anytime during the following two weeks so it was agreed he would travel to Top Meadow on Wednesday 26 July. He hoped to be able to meet Hilaire Belloc in London on the way and attempted to set up an appointment but due to lost addresses and wrong addresses, the meeting for the Monday afternoon was not confirmed. Father O'Connor waited patiently for him at Westminster Cathedral at what he thought was the appointed time but Belloc never came. Father O'Connor then had a day and a half to spend in London before going down to Beaconsfield. When he and Belloc did eventually catch up with each other some weeks later, Belloc admitted he had particularly wanted the meeting in order to deter Father O'Connor from meeting Chesterton, believing he would never become a Catholic.

The day after being summonsed to Beaconsfield, Father O'Connor informed his bishop in Leeds that Chesterton had written asking him to go to see him and he thought this was in connection with his being received into the Church. Personally he still doubted Gilbert would go through with it but thought he ought as he had been instructing himself long enough! Father O'Connor had already requested the appropriate forms from the Bishop of Northampton, Dudley Charles Cary-Elwes, just in case the hoped-for event did indeed take place. The latter was rather over optimistic as he also sent some blank forms in case Frances, or anybody else there, felt the urge to convert! Father O'Connor requested his own bishop to let him make his retreat at Douai instead of the general one at Mount St Mary's College in Chesterfield due to the time factor.

When Father Ignatius Rice, headmaster of the school at Douai Abbey in Woolhampton, heard the news of the pending conversion from Father O'Connor, he was overjoyed. Ever since the publication of *The Defendant,* Father Rice had devoured every word written by Chesterton 'almost with sacramental reverence'.[7] He suggested Chesterton be received at Douai Abbey, if not, would he at least visit them with Father O'Connor when he went there on retreat. If he could be persuaded to come, Father Rice offered to send a car to collect them both and take Chesterton back to Beaconsfield. As is well known however, the long-awaited event took place in the somewhat less than holy surroundings of the Railway Inn, which somehow seems appropriate, as Beaconsfield didn't have a Catholic church until four years later.

The morning after Father O'Connor's arrival at Beaconsfield, he was returning from the village with Frances when he told her that Gilbert's main concern about his conversion was the effect it would have on her. She replied that after three trying months with a very fidgety Gilbert, she would be greatly relieved. God had not yet chosen to show her the way clear enough to justify the same step for herself, but when he did she would be only too glad to join her husband.

Father O'Connor was thus able to reassure Gilbert in the afternoon of his wife's acceptance of the matter. They went on to discuss special points which still troubled Chesterton, but the priest then left him alone to read through the *Penny Catechism* to make sure there were no further troublesome obstacles. Gilbert spent the next day wandering in and out of the house, carefully pondering the catechism but no further problems arose. On Sunday, 30 July 1922, they set out for the dance room of the Railway Hotel, Gilbert choosing a beautiful snakewood stick, given to him by the American Knights of Columbus, to accompany him on the short walk that would mark the end of a very long journey. Belloc considered Chesterton's conversion to have been both deliberate and mature, as having once looked with interest at the Catholic Church from a distance, he gradually approached by a direct road before finally choosing to enter.

As Chesterton had not accepted the invitation to Douai, Father Ignatius Rice went to Beaconsfield to witness the ceremony. Frances was there of course, in tears, which Father O'Connor liked to believe were not all of grief. She took Father Rice back to Top Meadow for tea while Gilbert and Father O'Connor went off to the village for tea with Lady Ruggles Brise. The latter was married to the prison reformer Sir Evelyn Ruggles Brise and as Gilbert had a relative, Captain George Laval Chesterton who had also worked on prison reform, the subject was naturally a topic of conversation. Before her marriage, Lady Ruggles Brise was the widow of the fourth Lord Camoys, Francis Stonor, related to Archbishop Stonor, himself son of the third Lord, who had ordained Father O'Connor in Rome, so they too had something to chat about.

Father O'Connor thought Gilbert was uncommonly quiet that afternoon and hoped that he himself had not talked too much, not that it would have been the first time if he had, he admitted.

Father O'Connor and Father Rice vowed to say nothing to the press about Chesterton's conversion and it was some time before the news became public. Responsibility for this lay with nineteen-year-old Gregory Macdonald, ex-pupil of Father Ignatius, who telephoned the *Evening Standard* as soon as he heard the news from Father Bernard Ryan at Douai. Father O'Connor received a brief reply paid telegram from the office of *The Tablet* on 10 August, asking if news of Chesterton's reception was correct. The cat was now well and truly out of the bag.

Much has been written about the effect of Chesterton's conversion on both himself and the wider public, but Father O'Connor now found himself being sought after to be congratulated on his part in the event for which so many prayers had been offered. Hilary Pepler expressed his delight by comparing Father O'Connor to a fisherman whose story of the big fish he had caught in his net would be the only story told in many gatherings for many evenings to come. He was much less effusive in his letter of congratulations to the big fish himself ending 'This is a dull letter considering the Te Deum in my heart.'[8]

On 12 August, Hilaire Belloc wrote to Father O'Connor [9] saying how he had been overwhelmed by the very great news. He had never thought it possible and was still 'under the coup of Gilbert's conversion'[10] a few weeks later. Only two days later he ended another letter by saying that the more he thought about it the more astonished he became.[11]

Bishop Cowgill of Leeds was delighted with the good news, of course, and hoped Mrs Chesterton would soon follow. Father Joseph Keating, parish priest of Holy Rood Church at Watford in Hertfordshire and whose father owned and published *The Tablet*, thanked Father O'Connor for his note and thanked God for the happy event, promising to pray for Mrs Chesterton's conversion. Frederic William Keating, the Archbishop of Liverpool, also thanked God for the grace bestowed on GKC and for the influence his conversion was likely to have on literary circles. He hoped he would be spared many years to serve the Church from within which he had frequently and generously vindicated while still outside the fold. He sent Father O'Connor his heartiest congratulations on his own part in the event.

Cardinal Francis Bourne, Archbishop of Westminster, thanked Father O'Connor for the good news and congratulated him on being God's instrument in bringing about the happy result. He would not forget to pray for Mrs Chesterton. Cardinal Merry de Val who was suffering a shade temperature of 101 degrees in Rome, felt it a real comfort to know that Chesterton's conversion, so long prayed for, had come at last. He too hoped Mrs Chesterton would soon follow.

Father Vincent McNabb thanked Father O'Connor for the good news of what he called 'Gilbert's homecoming'[12] but understood at what cost the tremendous step had been taken. Though his friends' patience had been tried by the length of time Gilbert had taken to make the move, the fact that Frances had not gone with him, proved that Gilbert must now have been set on doing God's will. To have left Frances behind had caused Gilbert great pain and would continue to do so until she felt able to join him, but Father McNabb felt her problems were psychological rather than logical, her vision being clouded by the suicide of her brother soon after his own conversion.

Prayers for Chesterton's conversion had been offered by many who were unknown to him, as a letter which Father Ignatius Rice received many years later, in 1945, revealed.[13] Father Ignatius had loaned his first edition copy of *The Ball and the Cross* to Dame Felicitas Corrigan, a Benedictine nun at Stanbrook Abbey who wrote that after she had read the fine passage on virginity in chapter eight, she found it unbelievable that Chesterton was not a Catholic at the time of writing. When Father Ignatius had given the nuns a talk on Chesterton's conversion, Dame Felicitas had been tempted to tell him that his own and Father O'Connor's prayers had been backed by the prayers of many others. She recalled her own schooldays in

Liverpool where her class-mistress, a young nun, made them solemnly pray each morning that somebody would physically carry GKC over the threshold of the Catholic Church as he was too lazy to get there himself. Their teacher maintained that once inside the door he would become a Catholic on the spot. The teacher did not live to see the realization of her hopes. It seems it was obvious to those who knew him personally or through his books that he naturally had the mind of a Catholic and they were only waiting for the inevitable to happen.

Some religious went further than mere prayer. A nun at Carisbrooke Priory on the Isle of Wight offered three years of suffering in addition to her prayers for Chesterton's conversion. She did not live to see the result of her prayers as she died in 1914. Father Bernard of Blackfriars Priory, Oxford brought Father O'Connor news of this great devotion to the cause, adding that he would ask their nuns at nearby Headington to pray now for Mrs Chesterton.

Robert North Green-Armytage, a Weston-super-Mare barrister and book collector, wrote to his 'dear friend and mentor' that he was glad to hear the 'glowing news' of Chesterton's conversion,[14] and was especially pleased at the part played in it by Father O'Connor. He hoped and believed that Mrs Chesterton would soon follow her husband and assured Father O'Connor that he could always rely on his prayers for any of the priest's intentions. Green-Armytage wrote a *Ballade of Homecoming*,[15] which contains the lines

> For 'Father Brown' sends news of note today
> That, from the foggy bogs of Fleet Street come,
> Within the Household of the Faith to stay,
> Our Chesterton hath found the Path to Home!

This had been suggested by Wilfrid Meynell 's article in *The Tablet,* entitled 'The Homecoming'.

News of Chesterton's conversion crossed the Atlantic, of course, but so too did Father O'Connor's own part in it. He received a request for a photograph of himself from George Barnard,[16] of the National Catholic Welfare Council in

Chicago, who syndicated a page of Catholic news pictures every week. Barnard had already used a photograph of the man himself, but felt a picture of Father O'Connor would be of great interest. He added how millions of Americans were tremendously pleased by Chesterton's conversion as he was a man they held in high esteem. According to George Barnard, in America legend had it that Father O'Connor was Father Brown, whether this was true or not he did not know but thought it good enough to be true. His own view was that there was a least a germ of truth in the story so that was how he had introduced the picture.

After the publication of *Father Brown on Chesterton,* Father O'Connor received a letter from a Frederick Headon[17] who had just bought the book and found it very interesting. He had lived at Beaconsfield and served Mass at the Railway Inn in Father Walker's time. He recalled travelling by train to High Wycombe with Chesterton on 24 September 1922, the day he was confirmed, privately after the main confirmation service, by Bishop Cary-Elwes. Headon was Master of Ceremonies that day and travelled back with GK to Beaconsfield. He regretted that he couldn't recall what they had talked about.

Gilbert Chesterton, and the rest of the world, had to wait another four years before Frances felt herself able to follow her husband into the Catholic Church. Father O'Connor had the first intimation that she was seriously on her way in a letter he received in June 1926.[18] She did not want to take instruction in Beaconsfield as she felt people would accuse her of only converting because of Gilbert, when the entire opposite was true and she had fought against this influencing her decision. Tired, worried and in poor health, she prayed that Father O'Connor, Padre as she now addressed him, would tell her what to do.

By July, Frances had decided it might be better to take instruction with Father Walker after all. With the many crushing problems with which she had to contend, it was difficult for her to find the time to take instruction and think things through; she begged her dear Padre to be patient with her. A few weeks later she had written to Father Walker[19] to make an appointment to see him and have a talk, after which, she felt she would know what to do.

The situation was finally resolved on 27 October when Frances was received into the Church at High Wycombe, and confirmed in the Cathedral at Northampton in December. Unfortunately, Father O'Connor was not able to be present on either occasion. Though she felt it had been a terrible wrench having to part with many memories and traditions, she was happy at last but she did want Father O'Connor to pray that she would make a good Catholic.

Notes

1. Chesterton, F., *Letter*, 16 October 1914, 102, British Library.
2. O'Connor, *Father Brown on Chesterton*, p. 94.
3. Ward, *Letter*, 30 December 1914, 105, British Library.
4. O'Connor, *Father Brown on Chesterton*, pp. 94–5.
5. Chesterton, G. K. *Letter*, Xmas Eve., 1920, British Library.
6. O'Connor, *Father Brown on Chesterton*, p. 125.
7. Rice, *Letter*, 20 July 1922, 87, British Library.
8. Pepler, *Letter*, 49, n. d., ibid.
9. Belloc, *Letter*, 12 August 1922, 69, ibid.
10. Belloc, *Letter*, 23 August 1922, 70, ibid.
11. Belloc, *Letter*, 25 August 1922, 71, ibid.
12. McNabb, *Letter,* 2 August 1922, 84, ibid.
13. Corrigan, *Letter*, 19 September 1945, Stanbrook Abbey.
14. Green-Armytage, *Letter*, 10 August 1922, 80–1, British Library.
15. Green-Armytage, *Ballade of Homecoming*, papers of John O'Connor.
16. Barnard, *Letter*, 31 August 1922, 65, British Library.
17. Headon, *Letter*, St Luke 1937, 88, ibid.
18. Chesterton, F., 'Letter', 20 June 1926, Ward, *Gilbert Keith Chesterton*.
19. Chesterton, F., 'Letter', n. d., ibid.

Chapter 9

1930s: Writing and Speaking

Part 1: Writing

Father O'Connor was a prolific writer, contributing many articles to *Blackfriars,* from 1921 onwards, and other journals on a range of subjects including a number of book reviews. However it was the French poet, playwright and diplomat, Paul Claudel, who most occupied Father O'Connor's literary talents during the early 1930s, beginning with his translation of *Le Soulier de Satin, ou le Pire n'est pas toujours sûr.*

The author, who was French Ambassador to Washington at the time, had collaborated with Father O'Connor on his translation, which was published, both here and in America, in 1931 under the title *The Satin Slipper; or, the Worst is not the Surest.* Father O'Connor admitted he had been anxious to begin translating the work almost before he had read it all the way through, only later did he realize the magnitude of the task he had undertaken and was thankful for the encouragement of Paul Claudel himself.

Claudel was a prominent figure of French Catholic literature in the early part of the twentieth century but had earlier lost the Catholic faith of his childhood through influences at university. His faith had returned to him in a flash of Divine Revelation on Christmas Day 1886 in the Cathedral of Notre Dame in Paris, about half-past three in the afternoon to be precise, according

to Father O'Connor speaking to the Catholic Conference of
Higher Studies at Ampleforth Abbey.[1] *The Satin Slipper* is a
vast work, in which Claudel took the whole world as his stage
and the constellations as the roof of his theatre. Two readings
of the book were scarcely enough to grasp the scope of the
work, as Frances Chesterton had found after Father O'Connor
recommended it to her. He assured her she wasn't being as
stupid as she felt herself to be, but was indeed in good company
as the majority of the members of the Académie Française, of
which Claudel himself was a member, had confessed to being
out of their depth with his work. Frances persevered and, two
years later after a third reading, she had learnt to love the book.

Prior to the publication of *The Satin Slipper*, Frances
advised Father O'Connor that he ought to get £100 down for it,
with a further £100 in advance royalties with ten per cent of
further royalties. Whether he received this we don't know as
she added that translations, though the most difficult literary
jobs, were very badly paid. Frances was coping with
ecclesiastical problems at the time, caused by their priest being
almost impossible to deal with and everyone trying to hear
Mass somewhere else. As she hated going outside the parish if
it could be avoided, she was looking forward to the spiritual
opportunities afforded by their forthcoming visit to Notre
Dame University in America where Gilbert was to lecture.

Claudel's first drama, *Tête d' Or*, or *Golden Head*, first
written in France in 1889, was re-written in 1894–5 at New
York and Boston. *La Ville L'Échange*, or *The Town*, was also
first written in France, in 1890, but a second version was
written in China seven years later. Claudel often re-wrote
important works; some of his plays were re-written more often
than they were produced. Father O'Connor discussed the two
plays in articles for *Blackfriars* in 1937[2] in which he reminded
readers that *Golden Head* was written before Claudel publicly
professed his conversion, while *The Town* followed the solemn
proclamation of his conversion. The latter continued the first
drama, of a man alone with his nothingness, with the
Commonwealth of Men completing it on a higher plane. Father
O'Connor commented that this spiritual sequence of the Higher

Logic appeared in all Claudel 's great plays. *L' Annonce faite à Marie*, or *The Tidings Brought To Mary*, was the subject of a short piece in *G. K.' s Weekly*. [3] Father O'Connor considered this to be more of a problem play than a great play and not at all in the same league as *The Satin Slipper*. Only a quarter of its length, this is a tale of two sisters: one dedicated to the flesh, the other to the spirit.

Paul Claudel collaborated again with Father O'Connor on the latter's translation of *Positions et Propositions*, a selection of Claudel's essays, of various lengths and on a wide range of subjects which appeared in English under the title *Ways and Crossways*. *The Physics of the Eucharist* is a long essay which deals in three parts with *What Remains after the Consecration, What is Changed after the Consecration,* and *What is New after the Consecration*. *The Third Meeting* (John 21:1–14) is that between Jesus and the disciples after his rising on Easter Sunday and is a much shorter piece.

Father O'Connor had discussed the subject of confession with G. K. Chesterton on one of their moorland walks, explaining how hearing confession was pretty boring for the priest, there being only ten commandments and three or four ways of breaking them. Just occasionally there would be a rare thrill as a soul emerged from the dark night into the light of morning, but more often than not the confessor became half-dazed from the constant repetition of similar sins, not to mention numb from the knees down. Some thirty years later, in October 1934, Father O'Connor translated Claudel's stark poem on confession and, when this was published in *G. K.'s Weekly*, added verses entitled *From the Priest's Side* in which he expressed these sentiments. [4]

A regular visitor to Father O'Connor's presbytery, during the period he was busy translating Claudel, was Hugh Ross Williamson who was then a journalist on the Leeds-based *Yorkshire Post* newspaper. He enjoyed coming to Bradford in order listen to the priest's wisdom, to learn of his beloved Claudel, and to enjoy looking at Eric Gill's Stations of the Cross, which he considered finer than the Westminster ones. Occasionally Williamson liked to try to argue with the priest.

One afternoon, he remarked that the doctrine of Hell was incompatible with a God who was All-Powerful and All-Loving. He was surprised when Father O'Connor retorted, somewhat angrily, that if Williamson knew what he did about the sins of Yorkshire business men, he would learn to thank God for the doctrine of Hell, even in its most literal interpretation. It was not until after he had become a politician that he saw the implications of this, that it was indeed the love of money that was the root of all evil, rather than money itself. The cheating ways of many, but certainly not all, Bradford textile manufacturers were well known among those they employed. Son and grandson of Nonconformist ministers, Williamson became an Anglican clergyman before converting to Roman Catholicism in 1955, after Father O'Connor's death.

In February 1932 a collection of Father O'Connor's *Poems: original and derived* was published. This is a collection of fifty-three poems, some of which had been written or translated for the *Arundel Hymns*. Others later appeared in *A Daily Hymn Book*, published in 1949, a small hymnal especially for use in Catholic schools, small churches and convents. Father O'Connor wrote a further three translations and an original hymn to a German melody for this later work. The Chestertons were delighted to receive a copy of the poems. Frances especially liked the poems entitled *St Michael, St Patrick,* written for the *Arundel Hymns*, and that of her own feast day, *All Saints*, while Gilbert was attached to *Villequier,* Father O'Connor's translation of Victor Hugo's poem *A Villequier.* The much shorter 1938 edition of the *Poems: Original and Derived*, contains a number of different poems to those in the earlier edition including translations of Flemish and Provençal carols and an Ode from book three of Horace rendered into Irish and entitled *To Lizzie.*

Richard Crashaw was a seventeenth-century English poet, son of a Puritan minister who had leanings towards Catholicism – not a healthy religious choice in Cromwellian England – so Richard fled to France where he was free to convert. His poetry was influenced by his reading of Italian and Spanish mystics and had an obvious appeal to Father O'Connor who translated some of his religious poems from the Latin into English verse.

Father O'Connor next turned his attention towards the liturgy and 1939 saw the publication, by the Catholic Truth Society, of his translations of the *Collects and Prefaces* from the Latin Rite Missal. In the Introduction he is quite scathing of inaccurate translation, often corrected but not generally adopted by authority, and cites the *Salve Regina*, a monument to slipshod enthusiasm about which some bishops fretted, though not enough to bring others into line. He also avoided using two or three words to translate only one, something Cranmer tended to do and which was admired by those unfamiliar with the austerities of the Latin language.

Ghost stories always had a fascination for Father O'Connor and he was a great collector of those he believed to be true, while he detested those he knew to be fakes. Some of these true stories he put together and submitted to Frederick Muller Ltd, publishers of his book *Father Brown on Chesterton*. The reply was not very encouraging. In their present form they were considered too Catholic for general consumption, while to reach a wider audience and attract more sales they required some re-working. They suggested that the reader who had submitted the report would be willing to undertake the task or Father O'Connor could do the work himself. He didn't like either suggestion so he decided to put the manuscript aside, which is how it came to rest, along with the letters of rejection, in the John M. Kelly library.[5]

Father O'Connor reported all the stories faithfully as he had no reason to believe that any of his informants were frivolous or inaccurate enough to be misleading. The stories convinced him that some people were born to see, others to hear; Father O'Connor admitted he hadn't the ability to see a ghost but there were occasions when he had heard, or even sensed one. For example, one afternoon he ran after the sound of a man's heels in the corridor of a church, even unbolting a door to follow them and only later realizing the futility of unbolting a door to follow what could not have passed through. After he had collected his surplice from the vestry he had a 'sudden fit of over-consciousness' while all extraneous noise 'sank into a chord of exquisite melancholy, like the first sweep of the wind on harp strings. I felt not unpleasantly sad and lonely, and distinctly very thoughtful and concentrated'. In this instance, Father O'Connor knew the place to be haunted, but he had a similar experience in one which, at the time, he didn't know had a ghost.

Ghostly experiences relating to the O'Connor family were included, as well as those told to him by both clergy and lay people. Father O'Connor relates tales of exorcism and exorcists, including the form which the exorcism should take, gives examples of poltergeist activity, and three stories where the Blessed Sacrament was inexplicably withheld from a dying soul. The most impressive story of all concerns Divine intervention and was told to him by an old priest, referred to only as Ethelbert, who had never told it to anyone else, but felt that Father O'Connor would understand. One Christmas morning, Ethelbert was on his way to say Mass eight miles away in a country chapel where the Blessed Sacrament was reserved. After cycling six miles he suddenly remembered that he had not brought any small particles for the people's Communion and had a vague recollection that only eight had been left over from the previous Mass. With no time to return for them he had to cycle on. When he asked the congregation of forty how many were intending to communicate, he was horrified for once to see that all of them intended to do so. During Mass he thought how he was to distribute Communion with only eight particles too small to be broken further. No solution came to him so he was forced to take the ciborium out of the tabernacle and at that very moment something told him to neither look nor count but just go on.

Ethelbert went on to give Holy Communion to those forty people with a full particle when he was quite sure there were only eight. He seemed to be taking it out of his own breast, he told Father O'Connor, but it left him in quite a state. The only proof he had that anything extraordinary had occurred was the awful prostration in which he lay for three days afterwards. The priest was in good company for it is said Don Bosco had a similar experience.

He might not have succeeded in having his ghost stories published, but Father O'Connor did have a part to play in a ghostly tale broadcast by the BBC in November 1937.[6] The story of *The Haunted House* was told by a young actress, Ruth Wynn Owen, who lived in a house which had been divided up into flats and which she shared with an actor friend and an artist. In the beginning she only heard footsteps and the front door being violently opened and her housemates were sceptical until they heard it for themselves. The top flat of the house was empty for some time before a new tenant moved in, only to be murdered a few weeks later. The ghost then became very lively and noisy, scaring the pet cats, making them bolt, their fur standing on end. The ghost also became visible to Ruth, leaving her more surprised than scared when she realized she could see right through it to the garden path and gate as it flung open the door. The actress and her friends eventually moved out but the new tenants, who knew nothing of the previous haunting, were affected even more deeply, violently in fact. One girl was found to be suffocating after having felt something pressed over her face, another was found unconscious after choking from having ghostly hands around her neck, while a third met the ghost on the stairs.

When Ruth's tale had been told, Father O'Connor was introduced to offer his observations and deemed the story to be true rather than false for a number of reasons. He suggested ways and means of disposing of the ghostly presence, one of the easiest being to put up a crucifix or other sacred emblem, a method G. K. Chesterton himself had used to rid his secretary, Nellie Allport, of a ghostly presence. She had recounted the story one evening when he and Father O'Connor were discussing haunted houses. On the very first day she had moved in to her new flat she felt someone had followed her from the front door, and continued to have the feeling of someone constantly looking over her shoulder. Being an agnostic and not believing in such phenomenon, she made light of the whole matter until one night when the ghost became extremely noisy, keeping her awake all night with banging on the door. She was not too afraid to check if there was anybody about, inside or

out, but there was no one. Looking very haggard at
Beaconsfield next morning, Gilbert had commented on her
appearance so she told him what had happened. He took her out
straight away and bought her a crucifix, with instructions to
nail it on the inside of her door. After doing this she was no
longer troubled and continued to live in her flat which, at the
time of buying, she had thought to be so cheap there must be a
catch in it, which, as she discovered, there was.

In his broadcast, Father O'Connor suggested other ways to
discourage ghosts but pointed out that not all hauntings were
evil; sometimes it was necessary to discover what it was the
ghost wanted. He gives instances, in his ghost stories, of
unhappy spirits wishing to right some wrong and not until this
has been done can the soul rest in peace. This method requires
the intervention of an expert in the matter, as does exorcism of
a haunted place or a person, both practices which Father
O'Connor was fully qualified to carry out. He included in his
manuscript the form of exorcism of places, which, he points
out, is cheaper than pulling the place down as some people
might suggest.

Part 2: Speaking

Father O'Connor included the prescribed methods of exorcism
almost a decade later when he addressed the Bradford
Athenaeum Society, one of the many local societies of which he
was a member, on *Diabolical Possession*. The club was
formed, in 1883, by Dr A. Duff, a professor of Hebrew and the
Old Testament, modelled on a club of the same name in
Montreal. Its purpose was to discuss and exchange ideas on
literary, scientific and philosophical subjects, while technical
subjects could also be discussed if treated in a literary and
philosophical manner. New members of the club were elected
by existing members, their number being restricted to
twenty-four who met in each other's houses, the host being
required to read a paper and provide refreshments. Father
O'Connor was elected in February 1923, and was club
president 1928-9, his presidential address, *The Nature and*

History of Tolerance, being greatly appreciated by those present in St Cuthbert's presbytery.

Remaining a member of the club until his death, Father O'Connor gave a dozen lectures during that time. He followed his presidential address with a talk the following year on *The Sudarium of Turin*. His love of the first Christians and hours spent in the catacombs during his years at the Venerabile, was put to good use with a paper on the early Christian cemeteries of Rome, enhanced by his use of lantern slides. Chesterton considered Father O'Connor to be one of the best Shakespearean critics and his love of Shakespeare was represented by a paper on *Hamlet*.

After the death of his beloved Gilbert, Father O'Connor spoke about Chesterton's philosophy with examples from his writings. Three months earlier, in January 1937, he had given the same lecture to the Link Society in Manchester, followed by lectures in February and March in Glasgow and Leeds respectively. The Librarian of Mudie's Select Library, a London subscription library with branches in Manchester and Birmingham, told him that the demand for books by Chesterton far outstripped what they were able to supply. Father O'Connor was certainly doing his bit to publicize the works of his friend. Included in his lecture was Chesterton's *Ode to St Michael in Time of Peace*, which first appeared in the *British Legion Book for 1929* but was later reprinted in *G. K.'s Weekly* in September 1936. Father O'Connor regarded the poem, which he included in *Father Brown on Chesterton*, as 'one of the high-water marks of religious contemplation'.[7]

At the end of 1937, the priest was again in Glasgow, this time as guest of Mr McGregor, vice-president of the Glasgow branch of the Chesterton Club. Father O'Connor was himself an honorary vice-president of the Club, of which Mrs Chesterton was Hon. Life President. At the dinner in May 1939 to celebrate the 500th meeting of the Bradford Athenaeum Club, G. K. Chesterton was again the subject of Father O'Connor's lecture. In his last lecture to the club in 1949, he discussed the poetry of Francis Thompson and Coventry Patmore, the latter a major nineteenth-century English poet and late convert to Catholicism. Coventry Patmore had also been the subject of a lecture some years earlier. Both papers, the result of mellowed reflection and the enjoyment of a long lifetime, were highly appreciated by the club members who were drawn into a discussion on the poetry of the subjects. As a member of the Catholic Poetry Society, Father O'Connor was well versed in the subject.

Unlike the Athenaeums, the members of the Bradford English Society, founded in 1920, were interested in the study of just one, or rather, two subjects, namely English language and literature. Lectures were monthly with study circles being formed for more detailed scrutiny of the subjects. These included Drama, Poetry, Prose and Philology, the latter including the study of dialect, Old and Middle English. The Bradford Playgoers' Society was associated with the English Society, giving members the opportunity to study both modern and ancient drama.

At the first provisional committee meeting of the English Society it was suggested that as G. K. Chesterton was to give the inaugural lecture he should be asked to be president of the society. Rather surprisingly two members of the provisional committee strongly objected to this on the grounds that Chesterton was not a fit and proper person to be president. Why he was not a fit and proper person, we are not informed but Father O'Connor and other members of this committee, not surprisingly, took exception to this remark. We can only imagine what discussion followed or how heated it was, but it resulted in this paragraph being crossed out. Instead, written in pencil, is a bland statement that after a general discussion other names were suggested, including H. G. Wells and Thomas Hardy. However at the first general meeting, and no doubt to Father O'Connor's delight, the proposal that G. K. Chesterton be asked to accept the position was carried unanimously and he duly became the first president. Father O'Connor remained on the committee until 1946 and a member until a couple of years before his death.

The president for the year 1922–3 was another friend, Hilaire Belloc. He replied to Father O'Connor's invitation saying how he would be greatly honoured to come to Bradford, the only problem being money, or rather the lack of it. He could barely afford the journey from Lindisfarne Castle where he was staying, as he would not be earning anything from the visit. He suggested that if the society were inclined to pay his expenses, he would come like a shot.[8] In a letter in the society archives, Belloc acknowledges receipt of expenses of ten pounds. As this letter is written on St Cuthbert's headed notepaper, it seems that travelling expenses had been paid and accommodation had been provided at the presbytery.[9]

Hilaire Belloc's presidential address was *The Making of English,* his thesis being that the English language was the latest of the great vernacular languages of Europe. In 1937, Father O'Connor himself tackled the English language when he gave a paper, entitled *The Scholarly Approach to English,* to a meeting of the Association of Convents and Colleges in London.

Father O'Connor was not a personal friend of all the notable presidents of the English Society but there was at least one more with whom he was on familiar terms, Sir Compton Mackenzie. One of the leading writers of his generation, his literary career covered fiction, travel, biography, essays, poetry and journalism but he is warmly remembered for his comedies of Scottish life. He came to Bradford in 1932 to give the Presidential lecture to the English Society, which, for this occasion, was in conjunction with Bradford St Andrew's Society and Bradford Caledonian Society. He took as his subject the author Sir Walter Scott, it being the centenary of the great writer's death.

Before the lecture, Compton Mackenzie was entertained to dinner at one of Bradford's leading hotels. He wrote that one of the pleasures of this visit was his meeting with Father O'Connor, who proposed his health.[10] In his response, Compton Mackenzie spoke of visits to Bradford by his actor father who told him that as he grew older he would realize that intelligence only began north of Nottingham. Perhaps this was because he found that Sheridan's play, *The School for Scandal,* took an extra twenty minutes to perform in Bradford than in

places south of Nottingham, as Bradford audiences appreciated
good plays more than most. This was bound to go down well
with Yorkshire folk as southerners were known to believe that
civilization ended, even further south, at Watford Gap. Hardly
surprising then that, as Compton Mackenzie said, the
Yorkshire papers were very good to him. Father O'Connor
must himself have made a good impression on him as he later
accompanied him on a visit to the girls of St Joseph's College.
Compton Mackenzie had become a Catholic when a young man
in 1914, before going to serve in the First World War as a
member of British Intelligence.

The society was not always able to secure the authors they
would have liked. Charles Rutherston was asked if he could
influence George Bernard Shaw to visit them but Rutherston
had never met the author, nor did he know anyone who had. He
did know that the late Mrs Steinthal knew him well so perhaps
Father O'Connor would be able to help if asked. Whether any
further action was taken is not recorded, but GBS was known
to the priest who referred to him as 'Barney Shaw'. Father
O'Connor was approached a few years later to request Maurice
Baring to address the society, but he had to report that Baring
was unable to come that year, nor did it seem likely he would
come at any other time. Father O'Connor's own lectures to the
club included those on Francis Thompson and Coventry
Patmore with a tribute to Chesterton at the first meeting after
his death.

Father O'Connor's culinary tastes are expressed in a letter to
the club secretary regarding a forthcoming supper, which he
wishes were more informal.[11] He suggests sardines and beer or
something tasty and Bohemian, perhaps meat pie with oysters
in it with beer or stout to drink, possibly a special claret cup
but this would more expensive and less British. He goes on to
suggest Irish Stew, a pig's head boiled with cabbage, turnip,
onions and potatoes for about four hours, which would be
consumed in considerably less time. It is unlikely that these
suggestions were taken seriously, but unfortunately it is not
recorded what was eaten at that particular supper.

There was one other local literary society, the Bradford

Pickwick Club, of which Father O'Connor was a member. A talk he gave one December about Christmas traditions, serves to illustrate his facility with languages. On the subject of carols he mentioned some French ones which appealed to him and launched into an unaccompanied solo. After this rendition in French, he sang his English translation before ending his performance with a comic recitation of the carol in a broad Yorkshire dialect. He told his audience how he had once been complimented on his Basque accent by a Spaniard who asked where he had picked it up. Father O'Connor had to tell him that he had made it up from the French, Italian and Spanish he knew but had followed the rules of the languages. A journalist who reported on the meeting had found it easy to understand why this cheery parish priest had been an inspiration to Chesterton.

Of course Father O'Connor also found time to indulge his love of art and, while still a curate at Keighley, he became a member of the Bradford Arts Club, just a couple of years after its founding by a few students from the Bradford School of Art. No records were kept of the early informal meetings which were held in a former hay loft, hence its original name the Loft Arts Club, over the workshop of George M. Atkins, a founder member of the club. Limited at first to only sixteen members, it was extended in 1906 by taking over part of the workshop. Anyone in sympathy with the aims of the club was eligible to apply for membership.

In the light of Father O'Connor's close association with Eric Gill and the Ditchling circle, still some years in the future, it is interesting to note how similar were the aims and ideas of the club. In an age of commercialism, it was felt that art was too often set apart from everyday existence whereas it ought to be an essential part of life with useful and necessary things being made beautiful. The rooms of the Loft Arts Club provided a studio and workshop for arts and crafts together with a meeting place for lectures, discussions and the exchange of ideas on both art and literature. Exhibitions were also held there from time to time, and in the exhibition which accompanied the opening of the extension, arts and crafts were a strong feature.

By the end of 1908 it was necessary once again to seek larger premises but funds fell short of the rent that was asked. This was partly solved by sub-letting to two further societies, but club member, Charles Rothenstein, not yet Anglicized to Rutherston, came to the rescue by paying the rent out of his own funds for the next three years. As a fellow member, Father O'Connor must have become acquainted at least with Charles Rothenstein long before he became a near neighbour and close friend.

An anonymous letter in a local newspaper in December 1915[12] complained of the number of unscrupulous Jewish picture dealers in Bradford who sold thousands of pounds' worth of spurious pictures, or at best cheap potboilers. Potential buyers were advised to look round the Bradford Art Galleries or at the Arts Club exhibitions before buying. With his uncanny instinct for the genuine article, Father O'Connor was unlikely to have been taken in by any such scam, as the writer of the letter seems to have been.

Father O'Connor remained a member of the Bradford Arts Club during his time at Heckmondwike so he would have had plenty of opportunity to expand his knowledge and keep up with current trends in the world of art, which would be useful when deciding on the best pictures to sell to raise funds for his new church. When he moved to St Cuthbert's he became even more involved with the world of art when he was invited to become a member of the Cartwright Hall Art Gallery committee. Being a member of the consultative committee which was responsible for the choice of exhibits at the Spring Exhibition, Father O'Connor was in an ideal position to start re- building his own art collection.

Amateur local artists were able to exhibit their work alongside recent work of leading British professionals at the shows, not always to the delight of the visitors. At the spring exhibition of 1931,[13] the deputy chairman of the Libraries Art Gallery and Museums Committee said there were some pictures in the exhibition that he wouldn't put in his backyard, and he was on the selection committee! The committee chairman admitted that they had opened themselves to a great deal of criticism but had weathered the storm and endeavoured to show Bradfordians every form of art from Pre-Raphaelite to the post-Impressionist. He added that they had the most progressive municipal committee in the country. The Deputy Lord Mayor of Bradford said the city had a great interest in literature, music and art, which its leading citizens (of which Father O'Connor was most definitely one) helped to cultivate, despite Bradford's reputation for only being interested in brass, as money was known in Yorkshire. It would appear some progress had been made in some quarters since Douglas Pepler had accused Bradfordians of only worshipping Mammon but, opening the Bradford Arts Club exhibition three years later in 1934, Father O'Connor spoke of the lack of sympathy that still remained on the whole between art and commerce.

For example, he thought that if an artist produced a world-shattering masterpiece some merchant would come along and, after a modest payment for the copyright, would churn out the masterpiece in such numbers that it would become merely a hateful eyesore. Father O'Connor would probably not be surprised today to see so many masterpieces being crudely reproduced on so many items of merchandise. Can one ever feel quite the same about the *Mona Lisa* after drying one's dishes with that enigmatic smile?

There was some hope for Bradford though. The Earl of Harewood, who opened the spring exhibition in 1932,[14] expressed the opinion that Bradford could make a substantial claim to be amongst the most progressive of cities that patronized the arts, possibly in the whole country. The exhibition was composed entirely of modern art, much of it very advanced and, as the Earl pointed out, it was not only painting that found a sympathetic reception in the city but also music and the others arts, making artists glad to congregate there. In such an atmosphere Father O'Connor would feel comfortable and at ease, able to indulge both the spiritual and cultural sides of his nature at home as well as on the national and international stage. It becomes clearer why he was content to remain a parish priest rather than seek higher office.

Whitelock's First City Luncheon Bar, also known as The

Whitelock's, the meeting place of the Luncheon Club whose members included Jacob Kramer and Fr O'Connor.

Turks Head public house and located in an narrow passage just off a busy shopping street in Leeds, was the meeting place of a number of Yorkshire personalities. Owned by the Whitelock brothers, Percy and Lupton, the latter being a flautist in the Leeds Symphony Orchestra, its seclusion gave it the atmosphere of a club accessible only to those who knew it was there. Those who did know included not only fellow musicians but also writers and artists, those in public office, medical students from Leeds Infirmary, and journalists, such as Hugh Ross Williamson, from the *Yorkshire Post* newspaper.

Jacob Kramer, the most prominent and regular visitor to Whitelock's, had come to Leeds from the Ukraine when he was

FATHER JOHN O'CONNOR
(G. K. Chesterton's "Father Brown")
BY
JACOB KRAMER

Portrait of Fr O'Connor by Joseph Kramer, from the *Heaton Review*.

eight years old, together with his Jewish parents, his mother an opera singer and his father a court painter. He studied at the Leeds School of Art before attending the Slade in London and becoming a major portrait painter of the internationally famous such as Pavlova, Ghandi and Eric Gill and, of course, Father O'Connor. In the later years of his life Kramer taught at both the Bradford and Leeds Schools of Art, the latter being renamed after him in 1968. He was at the centre of local cultural life, organizing lunches and dinners in honour of eminent visitors to Leeds. As Father O'Connor honoured Whitelock's only on more formal occasions, according to John Rothenstein,[15] he was likely to be a guest at many of them. Father O'Connor presided at a farewell dinner at Whitelock's on the occasion of John Rothenstein leaving his post as Director of Leeds City Art Gallery to take on Sheffield's new art gallery; Rothenstein later became Director of the Tate Gallery in London, which houses a bust of Jacob Kramer by his friend Jacob Epstein.

In June 1945, Father O'Connor received a letter[16] which, as an admirer of Mark Twain's writings, must have given him great pleasure. Cyril Clemens, a distant cousin of Mark Twain and founder of the International Mark Twain Society, had written to Father O'Connor with the good news that, in recognition of his outstanding contribution to scholarship, he had been unanimously elected to honorary membership of the society. Cyril Clemens, a lifelong collector of Mark Twain history, started the Society in the 1920s and began publishing the *Mark Twain Journal*. He signed up every famous person he could and a list of the Honorary Members appeared on the headed letter sent to Father O'Connor; Hilaire Belloc and George Bernard Shaw were there but no G. K. Chesterton while Jacques Maritain wasn't added to the list until some time later. Dukes and generals, including General Montgomery and General Eisenhower, were among those honoured with membership at the time of Father O'Connor's election, while the chairmen of the various committees included Winston Churchill, (biographical), King Leopold of Belgium (entomological), and General de Gaulle (military). The parish priest was indeed in illustrious company.

Father O'Connor was a member of a second club with an international membership, the Pontifical Court Club, about which there is very little information and, when I enquired, very few people seemed to have heard. The first reference to it came in a letter to Father O'Connor[17] amongst his papers in the John Kelly Library. This informed him that the forthcoming Annual General Meeting of the club would take place at Claridge's Hotel in London on 21 April 1949; an agenda was attached. The meeting was to be followed by the annual dinner when decorations (of which there were plenty) would be worn; clergy should wear ferriolas.

Research led eventually to the Talbot Library, the Lancaster Diocesan Library at Preston, and the Revd Michael Dolan who was able to produce a copy of the *Rules and List of Members* of the club for 1952–5. The club was founded in 1908, during the reign of Pope Pius X, and appears to have ceased sometime in the 1970s. Its members consisted of the English-speaking members of the Famiglia Pontificia who paid a single life membership subscription of three guineas, or ten dollars for American and Canadian members. Anyone who ceased to be a member of the Famiglia Pontificia automatically ceased to be a member of the club.

The Famiglia Pontificia, or Papal Family, included a wide variety of officials, from cardinals to a large number of chamberlains whose functions were mainly ornamental, including the group of privy chamberlains to which Father O'Connor was appointed in 1937. The appointment, which carried the title 'Monsignor', made him eligible for membership of the Pontifical Court Club. We don't know when he first became a member but he is listed as a deceased member in 1952 and it seems likely that he would have joined as soon as possible, his membership therefore being during the reigns of Popes Pius XI and Pius XII.

The two objects of the club were to further the interests of the Holy See, as far as was in its power, and to promote the social intercourse of its members. The annual dinner or lunch was to take place around the anniversary of the election or coronation of the Pope, and a High Mass was to be celebrated every year for the intentions of the Holy Father. The chaplain offered a Mass for the same intention on the feast, or hereabouts, of SS Peter and Paul and Masses for the deceased. For their part in furthering the interests of the Holy See, the Pontifical Court Club published the quarterly journal *Catholic Documents* which consisted entirely of translations of papal documents. The only other information they yielded was that the headquarters of the club was, for at least a time, at 31 Portman Square in London.

Apart from taking an active part in the cultural life of the city and beyond, Father O'Connor was not one to neglect his parochial duties and the 1930s saw him embark on building his second church. This was no ordinary church, as was only to be expected where Father O'Connor was concerned.

Notes

1. O'Connor, 'Paul Claudel', *Ampleforth Journal*, pp. 159–68.
2. O'Connor, 'Claudel, Dramatist', *Blackfriars*, pp. 126–30, pp. 257–61.
3. O'Connor, 'Problem Plays', *G .K.'s Weekly*, p. 352.
4. O'Connor, *Father Brown on Chesterton*, p. 11.
5. O'Connor, *Father Brown's Ghost Stories*, papers of John O'Connor.
6. Owen and O'Connor, *It Might Happen to You*, BBC script, papers of John O'Connor.
7. O'Connor, *Father Brown on Chesterton*, p. 135.
8. Belloc, *Letter*, 23 August 1922, 70, British Library.
9. Belloc, *Letter*, 27 September 1922, Bradford English Society.
10. Mackenzie, *Octave Seven*, p. 76.
11. O'Connor, *Letter*, 9 August 1924, Bradford English Society.
12. *Letter*, December 1915, Cartwright Memorial Hall.
13. *Newspaper Cuttings*, ibid.
14. Ibid.
15. Rothenstein, *Summer's Lease*, p. 207, p. 220.
16. Clemens, *Letter*, 1 June 1945, papers of John O'Connor.
17. Walsh, *Letter*, 31 March 1949, papers of John O'Connor.

Chapter 10

Father O'Connor Builds a 'Round' Church

After the First World War, the lifting of building restrictions led to a rise in housing development with a subsequent increase in the local population. In Father O'Connor's parish this meant that a growing number of Catholics were having to walk greater distances, often over rough paths and unmade roads, to reach the parish church of St Cuthbert. It soon became clear that what was needed was a chapel of ease, served from St Cuthbert's, to cater for the more outlying parts of the parish. Those living in the area set about raising money, with a success that this time didn't necessitate their priest selling his pictures. Of course with Father O'Connor in charge, it was no simple chapel that resulted but a church that reflected the Liturgical Movement on the Continent and was decades ahead of its time.

The site eventually purchased for the new church was not the easiest to develop, being on a very steep hill, with the average ground level being some eight feet below the adjoining road. To overcome the problem it was decided to provide a basement which would accommodate the choir's vestry, store rooms, toilets, and an assembly room. Father O'Connor chose a local Catholic architect, Jack Langtry-Langton, his brief being to design a building in which the Liturgy of the Word and the Eucharist would be clear and understandable to the congregation. Some years earlier in *Why Revive the Liturgy, and How?*[1] which was only circulated privately, probably because of the somewhat radical views expressed between its covers, Father O'Connor had written:

> The Liturgy is essentially and exclusively the solemn sacrifice of the Mass ... so that when we speak of reviving the Liturgy we speak of reviving the public celebration of Mass ... You cannot revive public worship until you have disinterred it, and it is buried a thousand fathoms deep. It is like a primeval forest long since turned to stone

During the course of one his Sunday sermons, Father O'Connor gave his view on the position of the altar, stating that to have it pushed to the far end of a long building with the priest turning his back on the people was an abuse which was 1000 years old. 'Fancy, if all representations of the Last Supper made Our Lord turn his back to the Apostles!'[2] He thought it unlikely that any reform would happen in his lifetime. He was right in that it was not until the reforms of the Second Vatican Council were generally adopted that the priest no longer turned his back on the congregation. In *Why Revive the Liturgy, and How?* which was probably written about 1928, his suggestions included many of the changes regarding vestments, language, the times and manner of communion, that would have to wait almost forty years to be implemented.

However, Father O'Connor was not prepared to wait for the rest of the world to catch up with all of his forward-thinking ideas. The correct placement of the altar was of great concern to him and he turned for guidance to the primitive Church where, with only small congregations, the celebrant would face the people as he stood at a central table, just as a host would face his guests. Consequently the altar must be in the middle of the place of worship, and that is just where he stipulated his architect should put it.

Jack Langtry-Langton's first design was based on a Greek Cross with a semi-circular dome, supported by eight columns forming an asymmetrical octagon, in the centre. This plan was similar to that of the Church the Holy Spirit at Heckmondwike, Father O'Connor's first foray into church building, but now, some twenty years later, it proved too expensive. It was back to the drawing board for the young architect who came up with a design not only more economical, but even more beautiful than the original. The octagonal dome, with a seventy-foot span, remained but now the whole body of the church was octagonal, almost round (which is how it is referred to locally). What was more exciting was the fact that there were no columns to hinder the congregation's view of both altar and pulpit, instead large raking piers were used to spread the concentrated roof load on the foundations at what would otherwise be weak points.

The doors, altar rails and tip-up chairs, the latter providing seating for just over four hundred and twenty, were of oak. Alms were collected by steel tubes connected to the basement as the church was open all day, often without supervision. The question of churches and their poor boxes was a subject close to Father O'Connor's heart and one he discussed with G. K. Chesterton on one of their walks on the moors. In *Father Brown on Chesterton*,[3] he recalled a church, to which he had once been attached, having its poor boxes broken into and large sums of money stolen because the boxes were not emptied for months at a time. To combat the thefts, the priest decided to keep the church locked all day. As Father O'Connor observed, that certainly kept the boxes empty. He thought all churches should have a crypt as not only was it handy for storing things, but it helped keep the building dry and the floor from rotting. He was acquainted with another church which had one of these chutes for alms but when they examined the contents they found some coins but almost as many spent matches, long hooked wires and pieces of string.

The foundation stone of the new church was laid on 2 June 1934, the opening ceremony taking place almost a year later on 28 May 1935. Father Keegan, one-time curate at St Cuthbert's, thought that Father O'Connor had managed to get away with building such a church because Bishop Cowgill was by then an old man who had not studied the plans too closely! In 1967 the Roman Catholic Metropolitan Cathedral of Christ the King was opened in Liverpool. At the time, John Carmel Heenan was the

First Martyrs' church, Bradford, exterior. Fr O'Connor's second church and the first 'round' church.

Father O'Connor (second from left) in procession at the laying of the foundation stone of the First Martyrs' church, Bradford, 2 June 1934.

Archbishop of Westminster but when the idea was first mooted he was Archbishop of Liverpool. He stressed the need for priest and people to be closely associated with the celebration of the Mass in accordance with the emerging pattern of liturgical reform, a traditional long nave was no longer acceptable as the celebrant at the altar was required to be seen by the congregation. To accommodate these new ideas, the architect placed the altar in the centre of the church and the seating on three sides, a design not dissimilar to that of a church in the Archbishop's previous diocese of Leeds. It seems the time had come for the world to catch up with Father O'Connor.

The name chosen for the new church in St Cuthbert's parish was the Church of the Martyrs of the Peace, but when medals were struck to commemorate the founding, the name engraved around a depiction of the new church was the Church of the Early Christian Martyrs. On the reverse a scene from the Roman Colosseum showed a group of early Christians about to be devoured by a lion. When the opening ceremony was performed by the Bishop of Lancaster, the Rt Revd Wulstan Pearson, the church had acquired a further name change to the Church of Our Lady and the First Martyrs. At first the church was served by one of the priests from St Cuthbert's, usually Father Eustace Malone, one of the curates; rarely did Father O'Connor say Mass in his new church. Just a few weeks after the opening, Father Bernard Blackburn became a curate at St Cuthbert's and early the following year, when First Martyrs became a parish in its own right, he was appointed its first parish priest. It was to this fellow Dowegian that Father O'Connor left his copy of the Ardagh Chalice on condition that he leave it to Douai Abbey, as referred to in the first chapter.

It was left to the Jack Langtry-Langton's son, Peter, working with Father James Lahart in the mid 1960s to finally bring the ideas of his father and Father O'Connor to fruition. The chairs, rails, altar and seating of the first design were all removable to enable the church to be used as a school or for meetings but, there no longer being such a need, plans were to be made to

First Martyrs' church, Bradford, interior.

make them permanent. Father Lahart was no less demanding than his predecessor but had a similar close relationship with his young architect. A new altar, sculpted from Santa Marina marble by Eric Redhead, the lectern and chair, occupied their original positions. The confessional was housed in the central arch of three but this was re-designed and became a small chapel to house the Blessed Sacrament. The tabernacle was now in the east end of the church, where Father O'Connor had always intended. The Blessed Sacrament altar was the gift of an anonymous admirer of Father O'Connor and provides a constant memorial in his unique church.

2006 saw a re-shuffling of the twenty Catholic parishes of Bradford. The textile industry was no more, the huge Victorian mills built by pioneers of industry were fast being adapted to become upmarket, very expensive, apartments, university student accommodation, offices and small businesses, even an art gallery. Apart from a general decline in regular church-going, the general populace had moved out to houses with gardens in the suburbs, and there was no longer a need for the very large, city-centre churches which were very expensive to heat and maintain. The number of parishes was reduced to ten and First Martyrs returned, for the first time since Father O'Connor's day, to being part of a joint parish with St Cuthbert's, but with a difference. This time St Cuthbert's lost its parish status and became a chapel of ease, with the newer and smaller church becoming the parish church with Mgr Philip Moger the parish priest. Together the churches form the parish of St Cuthbert and First Martyrs of Rome, yet another name change for the latter but one which Father O'Connor, with his love of the early Church, would surely approve.

In January 1935, Christopher Dawson, the Catholic historian and author, brought Eric Gill to Bradford to stay overnight with Father O'Connor in order to visit his new church and, almost as important to Eric, to fit in a visit to the pantomime at the Bradford Alhambra. Gill had been Dawson's guest at Hartlington Hall, between Appletreewick and Burnsall in the Yorkshire Dales, where he had been adding a Greek inscription to the cross he had carved as a memorial to Dawson's parents. Eric Gill and David Jones had been working on this carving at Hartlington at the end of 1934 and Father O'Connor had paid them a visit on a cold, snowy day in November. He had sent on ahead of him a fine salmon, 'for he was quite a gourmet', recalled Dawson's daughter, Christina.[4] She also remembered the time Father O'Connor and David Jones were dining on the

Gill's memorial to Chistopher Dawson's parents, Burnsall.

train en route to Bradford from London and the priest being so
displeased with the food provided in the dining car that he
suddenly hurled a plate of spaghetti at an astonished waiter.
The salmon must have been perfectly prepared by the cook at
Hartlington as Father O'Connor stayed on for tea before
returning to his parish. Christopher Dawson, who became the

first Stillman professor of Roman Catholic studies at Harvard University, is buried in the grave next to his parents in St Wilfrid's churchyard, Burnsall.

Soon after Gill was back at Pigotts, he wrote[5] to Father O'Connor telling him how he had enjoyed his brief visit, especially to the pantomime, *Red Riding Hood.* He was less happy about a letter he had enclosed from Father Vincent McNabb to whom it seemed he had given offence. Gill wasn't sure how he had offended him but had told him he was sorry if he had done so in any way. Father Vincent, he felt, had been uncharitable in thinking him wilfully perverse rather than simply mistaken in his opinions. An interview with Gill by the editor of the *Sun-bathing Review,* had subsequently appeared, together with quotations from Gill's *Clothes,* as an article in the winter edition. Eric had also enclosed a copy of the article and begged for the priest's advice and to know if he had said anything heretical or imprudent which might have accounted for Father Vincent's displeasure. He was overjoyed, a couple of days later, to receive the assurance as to the orthodoxy, decency and general 'o.k.-ness of the *S.-B Review* article'.[6]

During the visit to Bradford, Father O'Connor and Eric Gill had discussed a proposed statue of St John Bosco and its placement in the new church. After making preliminary drawings in February and March, Gill started carving the Portland stone figure on 11 April 1935, ably assisted by Anthony Foster, one of his most distinguished pupils. By mid-July, the statue was far enough advanced for Gill to carry out the remaining work in Bradford. He arrived at Father O'Connor's on 16 July and after four days work the figure was finished. Gill later remarked that the work was 'pretty good in some ways but a bit queer'.[7]

The statue shows the saint holding a book bearing the inscription MASSIME ETERNE, and accompanied by the mysterious protective dog, Grigio, which always went with him on dangerous journeys. There is no obvious link between the saint, who had been canonized the previous year, and the dedication of the church; the link, I feel, is rather between the

Gill's statue of St John Bosco, First Martyrs' church, Bradford.

priest who commissioned it and the saint himself. Poor young people, schoolchildren and students came under the saint's patronage and these were groups for whom Father O'Connor himself felt a great deal of affection and love. Amongst Father O'Connor's papers[8] is a poem in six verses entitled *St John Bosco* which, as no author is named, I assume he wrote himself. The poem expresses the Saint's love for lost children as:

> Then over him a mighty softness stole
> Of Fatherhood, to rescue from the mire
> Discarded children, outlaw'd of control,
> Or home, or food, or fire.

Eric Gill hoped that the arrangement of Father O'Connor's new church would win the general approval he felt it deserved. Personally he saw no hope for liturgical revival until every church had followed Father O'Connor's example and removed the sanctuary from obscurity and placed it in view of the congregation. At the beginning of 1938, Gill had been asked to help in the re-designing of the chapel at Blundells School in Tiverton, Devon. When Gill visited the school he gave the boys a lecture on Christian altars, which formed part of an article he had written entitled *Mass for the Masses* in which he insisted that the altar be placed in the centre of the church. He then designed a new altar for them, which the boys made, but, as it had not been feasible to put the altar in the centre of the chapel, they cleared the pews from the east end of the chapel and placed the altar in the centre of this space. Previously the altar had been some distance from the congregation at the end of a long nave but Eric Gill stressed that the changes were a matter of liturgical, rather than architectural, reform. Eric sent a copy of his article to Father O'Connor for criticism and, he hoped, for approval. After its publication, Gill was approached to design a church for Gorleston-on-Sea, near Yarmouth, incorporating a central altar and embracing his ideas on reform. About three months after Eric Gill had written his article he returned Father O'Connor's original booklet *Why Revive the Liturgy,* which he had been copying, apologizing for keeping it such a long time. He, meantime, had certainly been doing his bit to make sure Father O'Connor's ideas, on liturgical reform, reached a wider public.

In 1919, not long after Father O'Connor arrived at St Cuthbert's, he had discussed with Gill his idea for a pair of statues depicting Our Lady and St Joseph but he had to wait until the end of January 1935, before Gill finally promised a drawing of the Madonna without fail the following week. On 1 February, her birthday, Gill's daughter Joanna modelled for the drawing, which Gill continued to work on for the next few days but it was put aside as other work, including the *St John Bosco*, intervened. A rather larger, and more important, commission was the one Gill was carrying out on behalf of the British Government as a gift to the League of Nations in Geneva. So it was two years later, in October 1937, before a second drawing was made of Father O'Connor's Madonna and the Bath stone model begun in November. At the end of the month Gill spent five days with Father O'Connor at St Cuthbert's. They had decided the statue was to depict the Blessed Virgin Mary at the moment of her annunciation, looking towards heaven as she receives the angel's message, her right hand pressed to her genital area, a gesture first used by Gill in 1911 in a carving of the Madonna now in an American university. Father O'Connor described the Madonna as depicting, in her self-chosen title, the Handmaid of the Lord, going out to God body and soul.

The League of Nations sculpture was due to be finished by April 1938 and the central panel was in place by that date but the smaller side panels were not in position until August. Eric managed to fit in a visit to Bradford in mid April as he continued to work on Father O'Connor's Madonna which he wanted to finish in time for the Royal Academy summer exhibition. After the exhibition, the statue, carved from Red Mansfield stone, finally came home to St Cuthbert's to stand at the side of the sanctuary on what Gill described as 'that beastly round pedestal'.[9] This is no ethereal figure but one with which many of the parishioners could identify and be comfortable with as the Blessed Virgin, her head raised heavenwards, clutches the ends of her headscarf, the usual head covering of the local mill girls.

The following year Gill began drawings for the accompanying figure of St Joseph which was to stand at the other side of the altar but it seems they did not meet with Fr

Statue of Our Lady, *The Annunciation*, by Eric Gill, St Cuthbert's church, Bradford.

O'Connor's approval and he started again. The second design did meet with his approval but as Eric had work for Westminster Cathedral that would occupy him until Christmas, he would not be free until after that to concentrate full time on St Joseph.

In January 1940 the work was going ahead but the statue was

May Bateman's statue of St Joseph, St Cuthbert's church, Bradford.

destined never to be carved by Gill. He began to be unwell during February and continued with health problems throughout the year and died on 17 November, ending a long, and somewhat unusual friendship with Father O'Connor. A statue of St Joseph did appear at St Cuthbert's church, however, a couple of years after Gill's death and there has been

speculation as to the identity of the sculptor ever since. I was
very fortunate to come across possibly the only reference to
this in a letter which Father O'Connor wrote to Dame Werburg
Welch in November 1941.[10] Father O'Connor told her that the
statue to match the Eric Gill Madonna was being carved by
May Bateman of Edinburgh, helped by her husband if and
when he was on leave from the services, both being disciples
of Gill. He didn't say if she was carving Gill's second,
approved, design or if she had produced a new design. In
November 1942, Father O'Connor sent Dame Werburg a
photograph of the plaster model of the statue, which would be
of Red Mansfield stone to match the Madonna, or *The
Annunciation*, to give the figure its official title. St Joseph was
on his own 'beastly pedestal' by March the following year and
Father O'Connor, unlike some later critics, thought he looked
well and made a fitting husband for the young Virgin.

    With Eric Gill's death, Father O'Connor had lost what many
considered a somewhat controversial friend but his church held
many beautiful reminders of their friendship.

Notes

1. O'Connor, *Why Revive the Liturgy and How?* p. 2.
2. O'Connor, *Month of Sundays*, p. 34.
3. O'Connor, *Father Brown on Chesterton*, pp. 19–20.
4. Scott, *A Historian and his World*, p. 115.
5. Gill, 'Letter', 28 January 1935, Shewring (ed.), *Letters of Eric Gill.*
6. Gill, 'Letter', 31 January 1935, ibid.
7. Gill, 'Letter', 20 July 1939, ibid.
8. O'Connor, *St John Bosco*, papers of John O'Connor.
9. Gill, 'Letter', 29 December 1937, Shewring (ed.), *Letters of Eric Gill.*
10. O'Connor, *Letter*, 10 November 1941, Stanbrook Abbey.

Chapter 11

The Chestertons Check Out

After the excitement of G. K. Chesterton's conversion, his
mentor and friend saw less of him, though when the two did
meet their theological discussions covered what Father
O'Connor called 'the byways of theology'.[1] In October 1933,
he observed some change in the great man, his conversation
had become slower and his breathing laboured, but when they
met again in the spring of 1934, Chesterton appeared to be his
old self again. Neither of them knew that this would be the last
time that they would see each other, at least in this world.

Gilbert was busier than ever but, though his wife thought
that work didn't really hurt him, she felt he ought to slow
down. A visit from Dorothea Steinthal had brought her up to
date with what kept Father O'Connor busy in Bradford, but
Frances was anxious to know when he would be able to visit
them again. She knew that the building and opening of his new
church had kept him fully occupied during 1935 but, when
Frances wrote to Father O'Connor in February 1936,[2] she
wished he was there with them so they could talk face-to-face
about her concerns. Gilbert was so overwhelmed with
questions and letters requiring answers and with what she
regarded as a useless controversy with George Coulton
concerning Puritanism and Catholicism, that he was prevented
from doing his own work. Not only was Frances worried about
her husband, but she was also having to cope with difficult
family problems.

Ever since Easter 1936, Father O'Connor had been haunted by the thought that Gilbert was not flourishing physically, so when he was in Aldershot a short time later he decided to go on to Beaconsfield for an overnight visit. Unfortunately he found that the Chestertons were in France visiting Lourdes and Lisieux at the time, but he was later relieved to hear that Gilbert had benefited sufficiently from this visit to the Marian shrines to joke and sing on the return journey to England.

Sadly, the improvement did not last and by early June Gilbert was seriously ill but still with a fighting chance of recovery. As he slipped in and out of consciousness he was anointed and, in a lucid moment during the afternoon, given his Last Communion. Father Vincent McNabb sang the *Salve Regina* at his bedside, as was customary with dying Dominicans. The hoped-for recovery didn't happen and on 14 June, Frances sent news that her beloved Gilbert had passed away that morning at 9.50 a.m. In Bradford, the congregation at St Cuthbert's were praying for him at the Mass which Father O'Connor was at that very moment offering for him, as he believed God had intended. Some months later, Frances admitted to Father O'Connor that her prayers at Lourdes had not been answered in the way she had expected, but however hard it was for her to lose Gilbert, she felt they had been answered in the right way.

Frances hoped that Father O'Connor would be able to go to Beaconsfield for the Requiem Mass on the following Wednesday, but unfortunately this was not to be as his doctor ordered him to bed on the Monday with a bad attack of bronchitis. It saddened him that he was unable to attend the funeral but at least his illness had the unexpected bonus, as he told Frances, that the six newspaper reporters who had arrived on his doorstep that morning had been turned away empty-handed.

Father Ignatius Rice wrote to Father O'Connor from Douai expressing the dreadful loss they all felt, but that Father John would feel more than most. He commented on how GK had saved him from being 'an intellectual utter ass when I was a young adventurer in thinking at Oxford'.[3] He hoped Father John would put his precious memories of GK on paper.

Father H. E. G. Rope also sent a letter of condolence to

Father O'Connor[4] knowing what a special friend Chesterton
had been to him. Although Father Rope had not had the
privilege of such a friendship, he had talked to Chesterton once
at the house of Chesterton's cousin and had been struck by
Chesterton's humility and exceptional courtesy. He was sure he
was greatly loved by all who knew him.

Father O'Connor's regret at having to miss his beloved
Gilbert's funeral was amply compensated by having the
Archbishop of Westminster (Arthur Hinsley) request he should
sing the Requiem Mass for his friend at Westminster Cathedral
on 27 June. In the meantime, Father O'Connor planned to visit
Father Bede McEvoy in Liverpool where he hoped the sea air
would assist him to stop coughing and start singing. When he
conveyed the good news of the Archbishop's wishes to Frances,
he added that he would go on to Douai unless she would like him
to go back with her to Top Meadow. Although the death notices
he had read in the papers and journals had all been good, Father
O'Connor pointed out to Frances that none of them had told just
how much of Gilbert and his books might have been lost to the
world without her beside him.

It was a great comfort to Frances when Father O'Connor
accepted the Archbishop's request, at which he was ably
assisted by Father Ignatius as Deacon of the Mass, with
Chesterton's devoted Father Vincent McNabb as Sub-Deacon.
Father O'Connor went back with Frances as she wished him to
stay the weekend with her at Top Meadow, and on the Monday
Dorothy Collins drove him to Douai.

On 7 July 1936, Father O'Connor made the first of many
visits to Stanbrook Abbey where he had several talks with the
Abbess, Dame Laurentia McLachlan, and her nuns. During
their recreation time he had entertained them with many
Chesterton stories, including how Chesterton's big knife had
been a great favourite with him for over twenty years,
accompanying him on his trips abroad, where he slept with it
under his pillow. Rather embarrassingly, Frances had often to
retrieve the knife when Gilbert left the hotel without it. The
nuns had enjoyed being able to handle it when it was passed to
them under the grille which separated them from their visitors.

On his return home, Father O'Connor received a letter[5] from the grieving Frances telling him how she was finding it increasingly difficult to keep going. The feeling she was no longer needed by her husband was almost unbearable and the Mass she had said for him every week was, she felt, more for the repose of her own soul than his. 'Vex not his ghost' was an old Catholic saying, the priest replied,[6] meaning that hearing Mass and especially taking Holy Communion, was very comforting to the dead. For his part, Gilbert would help comfort her own soul as she prayed quietly for him. Only time would dull the edge of her pain but then Frances would come to realize the value of the work in which she had played such a great part.

In October 1936, *The Downside Review* carried an article by Father O'Connor entitled 'Gilbert Keith Chesterton, Only a Memory' in which he refers to his first meeting with Chesterton. He describes the occasion as it later appears in *Father Brown on Chesterton*, the meeting after the lecture on Modern Thought, of which no one has heard, and the walk over the moors on a blustery March day, which in reality took place on the previous December, as described in chapter three. The following year, *The Downside Review* published the substance of a memorial lecture which Father O'Connor had given to the Bradford English Society in October 1936. He told them that their past president had been a serious child who never grew up but was, nevertheless, one of the greatest essayists that ever lived.

After Chesterton's death, Father O'Connor paid many spoken and written tributes to his dear friend. Extracts from some of these are recorded in St Joseph's College magazine for January 1937 which reported the loss of 'their special friend by proxy'. One of these extracts is from an address by Father O'Connor to the Bradford Aquinas Society entitled *St Thomas Aquinas and GK*; He told them that St Thomas was said to have been a fat man; there was no doubt GK had also been a fat man, but there were less obvious affinities between the two. The saint, known for his courtesy, was known as the Angelic Doctor, while the courteous Chesterton could similarly be called the Angelic Jester. Chesterton had published, in 1933, what Étienne Gilson, the Thomist philosopher, considered the best book ever to have been written about St Thomas Aquinas, and one which, although he had studied the saint all his life, he could never have written. Chesterton's wit had made it a very readable book, expressing what scholars' academic formulas had failed to do. Chesterton dictated half his book to Dorothy Collins before asking her to go to London to buy books about St Thomas, but he had no idea what books she should buy. Dorothy immediately wrote to Father O'Connor for advice and he quickly obliged with a list. He also enclosed a letter from Father Godfrey Anstruther of Blackfriars School, Laxton, who had just sent Father O'Connor his translation of *Foundations of Thomistic Philosophy* by A. G. Sertillanges in return for Father O'Connor translating a verse of French poetry by Paul Valéry for him. When Dorothy obtained the recommended books, Gilbert read through them quickly before dictating the remaining half of the book without further reference to them.

In October 1936, Father O'Connor received a request from the BBC to give a ten-minute talk on Chesterton's forthcoming autobiography. In suggesting this, the programme director hoped he would review Father Brown, treating him as he wished, severely, leniently, analytically, or critically. He hoped Father O'Connor would allow them to announce that he was the original of the fictional character. Of course Father O'Connor was happy to oblige and when he submitted his script for scrutiny, the director made only one slight alteration to assist the flow of his words.

On 23 September 1937, *G. K.'s Weekly* called the publication on the same day of Father O'Connor's own book, *Father Brown on Chesterton,* 'an event of real literary importance'. Rather than being a formal biography, the book is more a collection of anecdotes which, more or less, follow a chronological order. Father H. E. G. Rope, who reviewed the book for *Pax*, found himself at the end of it wanting more and hoped that one day the author would write a fuller and less patchwork account of his friendship with Chesterton. The reviewer in *The Irish Ecclesiastical Record* had finished the book with similar feelings. He compared the author to his fictional counterpart, going about the work in a competent and very unobtrusive way but, just as Father Brown slipped away quickly after solving the crime, so Father O'Connor suddenly finishes the book leaving his readers waiting to hear more. Father Ignatius Rice appreciated the fact that the book gave an insight into how many of Chesterton's ideas grew from conversations, remarks or incidents which took place when the writer and the priest were in each other's company. I hope *The Elusive Father Brown* broadens that insight.

A second volume of memories of Chesterton never did appear nor was it ever contemplated, but Father O'Connor remembered his friend on the tenth anniversary of his death with 'G. K. Chesterton: Recognita Decennalia' published in the journal *The Nineteenth Century* in June 1946.

Frances tried to take up her life again after Gilbert's death and, when she visited Father O'Connor at St Cuthbert's shortly after, he took her to meet the Sixth Form girls of St Joseph's College who had been so impressed by GK when he had visited them. Frances, striving against indifferent health and weighed down by her recent loss, charmed them with her conversation and her simple manner. She recounted anecdotes about her husband but also discussed the merits and de-merits of the BBC and the future of television. When she visited the Juniors, she showed her great love of children and her delight at being with them. As they recalled her big, buoyant husband who was yet so child-like and dependent, and looked at the fragile restrained figure of his wife which concealed a shrewd and reliable personality, they concluded that their life together must have been a study in contrast.

Dorothy Collins nursed Frances Chesterton during her last painful illness, until she had to be moved into St Joseph's Nursing Home in Beaconsfield to be cared for by the nuns. In November, Father O'Connor sent an SOS for prayers to be said for her in all their schools, the children's prayers had done wonders for her in the past and he hoped they would do so again. They didn't have the outcome he desired but no doubt they helped her to bear her illness bravely until she was released from her suffering on 12 December 1938. Only two years after the loss of his beloved Gilbert, Father O'Connor lost another dear friend and one that brought to an end a correspondence that spanned over thirty years of shared sorrows and joys.

Notes

1. O'Connor, *Father Brown on Chesterton*, p. 150.
2. Chesterton, F., *Letter*, 10 February 1936, 153–4, British Library.
3. Rice, *Letter*, 15 June 1936, 158, ibid.
4. Rope, *Letter*, 16 June 1936, 160, ibid.
5. Chesterton, F., *Letter*, 21 July 1936, 166, ibid.
6. O'Connor, *Letter*, 23 July 1936, 167, ibid.

Chapter 12

1936–49: Enclosed Nuns and a World War

The visit to Stanbrook Abbey after Chesterton's death in 1936 saw the start of another great friendship, and another correspondence, this time between Father O'Connor and Dame Werburg Welch with whom he corresponded until his final illness in 1951.

Stanbrook Abbey at Callow End in Worcester was, at the time of Father O'Connor's visit, an enclosed Order of Benedictine nuns, who were, nevertheless, blessed with open minds. The grilles were removed in the early 1970s but the nuns themselves removed in May 2009 to a newly built, very modern abbey more suited to their twenty-first century needs. Situated in the beautiful surroundings of the North York Moors National Park, the nuns are near neighbours of the Benedictine monks at Ampleforth Abbey in an area once renowned for the wealth and glory of its monasteries. Though Stanbrook and Ampleforth may lack the wealth of their predecessors, their presence keeps alive the spirit of monasticism that once existed on the North York Moors.

Father O'Connor's visits to Stanbrook were affectionately remembered by the Abbess, Laurentia McLachlan, and her nuns.[1] He would entertain them with brilliant, if rambling, monologues while his adventures with GKC would be recounted in his best Father Brown vein and, of course, there would be the inevitable ghost stories. Both Father O'Connor and the Abbess had a wide range of friends, not necessarily of

the same, or indeed any, faith, and both showed a deep
understanding and compassion for their fellow human beings
from all walks of life. They shared a love of Gregorian chant,
though she was an authority on it and pioneered its revival in
England. With the same cheery countenance and a twinkle in
their eyes, it is not difficult to see how they would get on so
well together. Father O'Connor was also to discover that he
had much in common with Dame Werburg Welch, not least
their mutual friends at Ditchling about whom snippets of news
were exchanged in their letters.

Dame Werburg was born Eileen Grace Welch in Cheltenham
in May 1894 and entered Stanbrook Abbey in 1915. She
studied art before moving with her family to Bristol, where she
continued her studies at the Bristol Art School. Meanwhile her
mother became a close friend of Desmond Chute's mother, on
one occasion taking her two daughters on a tour of Italy with
Desmond and his mother. Desmond and Eileen corresponded
on wood engraving and in 1919, after he had joined the
community at Ditchling, he began to tutor her by post, at the
same time passing on to her Gill's social and aesthetic dogma.
Eric Gill first visited Stanbrook with Pepler to seek advice on
the printing of plainchant from the nuns who ran the Stanbrook
Abbey Press, the oldest private press in the country.

Dame Werburg was first introduced to Gill when he paid his
second visit to the abbey with Desmond Chute in July 1921. An
article in *L' Artisan Liturgique* [2] names her as one of two young
sculptors to be more or less influenced by Gill, and though she
was certainly influenced by him, she developed her own
variation of the Ditchling style in which her characteristic
elongated figures echoed her favourite Byzantine period. The
other sculptor mentioned with her was Dom Hubert von Zeller
of Downside Abbey, one of Dame Werburg's closest artist
friends.

A further link with both Father O'Connor and Ditchling
came through Aileen Clegg, who had grown up in the Keighley
parish of St Anne's where Father O'Connor was then a curate
and knew this Catholic family well. Aileen met Dame Werburg

through their mutual friend, Dame Scholastica Hebgin, with whom she had been at college, when she visited Stanbrook for Dame Scholastica's Solemn Profession. Aileen later married Philip Hagreen, a painter and wood engraver, and lived with him at Ditchling. In 1923, Dame Werburg discussed with Philip the possibility of publishing *The Revelation of Divine Love* by Julian of Norwich, illustrated with her woodcuts. Her designs were sent to Ditchling but the book was never published. Hagreen was also mentioned in the article in *L'Artisan Liturgique*, as a disciple of Gill who, together with Laurence and Joseph Cribb and Anthony Foster, were producing remarkable work.

Dame Werburg's productivity increased as she matured, with much of her sculpture being commissioned by Father O'Connor. The first letter in the collection[3] dates from October 1936, and is in answer to one from Dame Werburg thanking her for the samples she has sent. These seem to be ideas for a carving of St Barbara, as he goes on to describe a framed picture of the saint and says he will send the specification as soon as he gets hold of it. Unfortunately, as there is no further mention of the statue, it may never have been made. He also asked Dame Werburg to carve an ivory baby Jesus, to be laid on real hay in a manger, for the Christmas scene at St Cuthbert's. The whole affair was to be very elaborate, with the Nativity in front of a view of Bethlehem, painted by the local art master, and complete with lighting and a real fountain. Father O'Connor wanted to wow his youngest parishioners. No doubt it did. Father O'Connor was very fond of ivory and offered to send Dame Werburg some if she ever needed it for carving. Some time later he asked if she was interested in four ivory tusks for about five shillings, which, he assured her, he had obtained honestly.

Dame Werburg's work reached a wide public through being exhibited and she often showed wood engravings, oil paintings, carved crucifixes and vestment designs at the annual exhibitions of the Guild of Catholic Artists and Craftsmen. Father O'Connor assured her, in December 1936, that there was no hurry for the St Joan he had commissioned if she wanted to exhibit it.

No letters survive from 1937, and there are only two from 1938. The first letter of these assured Dame Werburg that she could use any verse of his that she liked for the Christmas card she was designing. The finished card bears a wood engraving of shepherds bowing down before the angels with their sheep alongside them, the accompanying verse appropriately entitled *Shepherd of the Mountain* which may be a translation an Old French Carol. Father O'Connor wanted some of the cards to send to his friends but wanted most of them to go on sale at the church door and asked Dame Werburg to send him as many as she thought him able to afford.

From Christmas card designs, Father O'Connor moved on to news of Desmond Chute, whom Gill had visited in spring in Rapallo, Italy, and told him how Desmond was a local swell and almost ran a Salon. Father O'Connor had also heard that Barney Shaw had been very unwell due to anaemia, which Father O'Connor put down to too much cabbage water in their diet! He ended his letter with a bit of medical advise for curing Dame Werburg's cough; according to an old doctor's remedy, drinking half a tumbler of milk to which five drops of iodine had been added would do the trick. If it didn't cure the cough at least it didn't harm Dame Werburg as she lived to be ninety-five years of age.

In the second letter from 1938, Father O'Connor requested Dame Werburg to offer the second volume of his poems to the Abbess with his unalterable devotion. The offer was taken up as the Stanbrook Abbey Library contains a volume inscribed 'To Mother Laurentia from John O'Connor. In the blest assurance that if she can stand Barney Shaw, she can stand him.'

In January 1939, Father O'Connor took a trip to Kylemore Abbey in Connemara, to attend the Golden Jubilee of the Abbess Maura Ostyn. He had been tempted by the invitation of an old friend of the convent, backed by the offer of a car ride across to the west of Ireland. The Abbess had brought the nuns from Ypres, after the abbey there was destroyed in the early days of the First World War, and had a difficult time before finally settling in Kylemore in 1920. Father O'Connor was very impressed, not only with the beautiful abbey, but how, with the help of the small school they had opened, by letting the fishing and providing board and lodging for visitors during the season, they had managed to reduce their debts considerably. On the journey back he and his travelling companions were involved in an accident when their car skidded and was badly damaged. Fortunately none of the passengers were injured and they were able to continue on to another appointment in Dublin.

Dame Cecelia Heywood, the Abbess of Stanbrook in the early 1920s, decided that it would benefit the establishment if her nuns learnt to spin and weave in order to produce the cloth for their vestments. Mary Ellen Boyd had met Val KilBride at Gospels, the home of Ethel Mairet in Ditchling village, before joining the Stanbrook community and becoming Dame Evangelista, so she was delegated to make contact with them. This resulted in Val KilBride being dispatched to Stanbrook in July 1924, where he stayed long enough to set up the weaving shop and give initial instruction to the nuns who were to work there. He returned to give them further help and advice in the following spring and KilBride silk continued to be used in Stanbrook vestments until the 1970s, maintaining the strong link between Stanbrook Abbey and the Ditchling community.

On the subject of liturgical vestments, Peter Anson wrote in *L' Artisan Liturgique*[4] that in Great Britain they had kept their traditional character more than in other European countries. It was rare to find examples which showed a tendency to break with the past as far as the form of the textiles and colours used was concerned and the Anglo-Catholics especially had contributed to the return of this popular medieval form. Considered as the pioneers of modern Catholic art in this domain were the Benedictine nuns of Stanbrook Abbey, together with the monks at Prinknash and Downside. Stanbrook vestments were less ample, but their beauty lay in the choice of colours and the embroideries which they were not afraid to make more lively and bright.

The first reference, in Father O'Connor's extant letters to Dame Werburg, to vestments being made for him at Stanbrook, comes at the end of March 1939. There had obviously been some discussions previously as he wanted the sleeves to be shorter and wider (none of the less ample style for him) and the skirt shortened. He agreed as to plain white but he wanted her to use a heavier linen and he could afford some frugal white lace on the sleeves and the skirt. He also ordered two albs.

The type of fabric used to make his vestments was of great concern to Father O'Connor and he considered having to wear vestments of the wrong texture to be a punishment worse than having to wear clothes lined with crumpled rose leaves. Accordingly, when he wanted an everyday set for winter weekdays he requested any bargains in cream for the decent price of fifteen pounds. He also required missal ribbons at sixteen shillings and sixpence as his 'economic stringency' was for the moment relaxed. The white vestments duly arrived and were worn on Trinity Sunday. They were very good and very cheap, but he complained that the veil was on the small side for the sort of Renaissance chalices he liked to use.

In *Why Revive The Liturgy and How*, Father O'Connor wrote that 'The chasuble must be of the stately and solemn nature that it was in the beginning – the vestment of the Orator or the Sage.'[5] After wearing the white chasuble on Trinity Sunday, he hoped that Dame Werburg would be neither startled or pained if he returned it for improvement as he has been told it didn't hang well, perhaps not making him look quite stately enough for his liking. On the last day of 1940, he enquired how much he would have to pay for fourteen yards of material for a white cope to match the white vestments already supplied. He added that it needed 'to talk', that is to be seen a long way off. Dame Werburg this time succeeded in meeting his stringent demands for he wrote that it had proved to be very effective when he wore it for the first time in their First Communion Procession six months later.

Dame Werburg was not the only supplier of vestments to Father O'Connor. Between 1930 and 1946, he also managed to keep the Coonan sisters, maiden ladies living in the parish, busy working for him. Their niece, who had been sent to live with them on account of her delicate health, recalled how Father O'Connor would breeze in with a roll of silk damask or similar material and a very clear idea of what he wanted, as Dame Werburg had discovered. Some of the material came from Stanbrook or Ditchling, but some he bought from his friend Ernest Busby, owner of a large department store where Bradford's wealthy élite shopped and lunched. Often Father O'Connor ordered orphreys from Dame Werburg to be used on vestments made in Bradford, anything from fourteen yards of her fifteen shilling kind to a peacock on a green background and a phoenix on crimson. Lively and bright colours to be sure.

Margaret recalled her aunts making the biggest cope she had ever seen. A semi-circle with a five-foot radius, white with an Old Rose coloured lining and an interlining of stiff canvas, it was capable of standing up by itself, taking up the tiny living room by so doing. To complete the piece, Father O'Connor produced a beautiful embroidered hood he had managed to procure from an Anglican church and which only required some slight adaptation.

Of course anything Father O'Connor had made would be highly individual. Margaret remembered two stoles in particular: one for the feast of Our Lady bore the embroidered initials MR and Tudor roses, while another for the Feast of Christ the King bore the initials IHS and a crown. The outline in gold was achieved by twisting a plain thread inside a fine Japanese gold thread and Margaret felt honoured when she was old enough to assist her aunts in this delicate task.

When Father Michael Magner, a curate at St Cuthbert's, moved to another parish, Father O'Connor presented him with three sets of vestments in white, red, and purple with a fourth reversible set, green on one side and black on the other. For one of the stoles, Father O'Connor decided overlapping falling autumn leaves embroidered in orange and light green would be attractive, so the Misses Coonan had first to produce a drawing of these which met with his approval before tackling the delicate embroidery.

The colours that may be used for vestments are laid down by the Church and blue was not an approved colour, so the sewing sisters were more than a bit surprised when Father O'Connor arrived one day with a beautiful roll of blue brocade patterned in gold. As the Spanish Carmelites wore blue for the Feast of the Immaculate Conception, he told them, he had decided he would too. This special privilege was extended to the English Benedictines as they were partly descended from the early seventeenth-century Spanish Benedictines. Downside Abbey have a set of blue vestments which are worn on the Feast of the Immaculate Conception in December, and in August on the Feast of the Assumption, though in the past there was a tendency to wear them on almost any occasion associated with Our Lady.

Father O'Connor would be well aware of this Benedictine practice but the small detail that this did not entitle himself to wear blue vestments wouldn't worry him too much. There was a problem though in that new vestments had to be solemnly blessed by the bishop and he might not approve of this bending of the rules. Father O'Connor solved this dilemma by slipping the blue vestments well down among others being blessed by the bishop, so passing them off blissfully un-noticed by his lordship.

Almost all the vestments made for Father O'Connor have disappeared but this famous blue one was recently discovered in a cupboard off the Chaplain's office at St Joseph's College. Margaret vouched for its authenticity from a photograph, even though she hadn't seen it for sixty years. The blue chasuble, lined with gold and edged with the gold cord so favoured by Father O'Connor, was completed by a beautiful red and gold orphrey designed and made by Dame Werburg at Stanbrook. The latter was recognized, from the same photograph, by Dame Anne Field of Stanbrook Abbey, who had worked with Dame Werburg in the Vestment Room at the time. The finished vestment is known to have been worn at least once for the Feast of the Immaculate Conception, but what reception and comments it received is not known. Not so the blue and yellow vestments worn by Pope Benedict to celebrate the birthday of the Blessed Virgin at Mariazell in September 2007, which attracted some very unfavourable comments and caused quite a debate on the internet as to when, and by whom, the wearing of blue vestments was permitted. Father O'Connor had once again been ahead of the game.

In May 1939, Father O'Connor stayed a couple of nights at Stanbrook Abbey and entertained the nuns with his traveller's tales. He gave a graphic description of his recent visit to Kylemore Abbey in the wilds of Connemara but was full of the cruise from which he had just returned. He had visited Iceland and Norway, venturing as far north as the North Cape. Iceland had appealed to him greatly, perhaps because he had been struck by how the Catholic Church was growing in that country and where a Catholic cathedral was in the course of construction just outside the capital, Reykjavik. In the North Sea they had met a Soviet cargo ship carrying pit props to Newcastle, probably from the Czar's own forests. Overloaded and listing badly to one side, Father O'Connor thought her symbolic of the republic for which her red flag stood. The account in the daily journal of the abbey describes Mgr O'Connor as having 'a genius for describing things in brief, almost desultory sentences', and it was only later his listeners realized 'what a depth of meaning lies in his words, leisurely as they are spoken with the richest of Irish brogues'.[6] Even so, with the Abbess confined to her bed and not there to draw him out, the writer felt they had not heard him at his very best.

One of Dame Werburg's most widely distributed wood engravings was of a figure of St Agatha, first commissioned by Father O'Connor in the early months of the Second World War. He sent her a photograph of a medieval St Agatha tile, the pre-Reformation style of fire insurance, suggesting she made a woodcut to produce prints to be framed and sold cheaply. If this could be achieved, he felt that Dame Werburg would be helping the war effort by putting out the incendiary bombs before they fell and set fire to their surroundings!

Fire prevention, earthquakes and volcanic eruptions all fall under St Agatha's patronage. A native of Catania in Italy, she was in prison, and, with her breasts cut off and having been rolled on live coals, was near death when an earthquake struck the city. In the destruction that followed the magistrate's friend was killed, causing the magistrate himself to flee. Thanking God for her release from pain, Agatha died. The medieval tile bore the inscription MENTEM SANCTAM, SPONTANEAM

HONOREM DEO, ET PATRIAE LIBERATIONEM. These words were engraved on a marble tablet carried by a youth who, with a band of followers, arrived in Catania on the day of Agatha's burial. When the funeral procession reached the burial place, the leader placed the marble tablet at the head of the grave. None of them were ever seen either before or after this event. A relic of her veil was used in 1886 to halt an eruption of Mt Etna, the lava stopping exactly at the spot where the approaching fire had been blessed by the relic.

By the end of April, Father O'Connor was in possession of 150 St Agatha prints; only five days later three dozen had been sold and in August they were sold out and more had to be ordered. He was very happy with the woodcarving and thought Dame Werburg had made St Agatha a masterful and valiant woman, and she should be sure to put her around the abbey.

Bradford suffered four bombing raids between 22 August 1940 and 14 March 1941. Father O'Connor reported to Dame Werburg that, during the first of these, three bombs were dropped and fell in nearby Heaton Woods, wide of any target. His ornaments had been shaken about though and it had sounded like someone was falling out of a bed above his ceiling. Minor damage and slight injuries to six people were caused by another four bombs which fell six days later. At the end of August, the third raid, during which 116 bombs were dropped on the city, killed one person and injured 111. The bombs missed the big engineering factories employed in war work, causing damage mainly to shops and department stores. The biggest fire gutted the department store of Asa Lingard, the art collector previously mentioned. The largest number of bombs were dropped during the last raid, almost 600, in March 1941, but did little damage to either people or property.

Father O'Connor had received another parcel of St Agatha prints just a few weeks prior to this last raid. The parishioners had great faith in her powers and the figure continued to sell well, which was no bad thing considering the sad state of the parish's defences against fire. Having only a stirrup pump with the ability to squirt water up to a mere five feet, an emergency required two fire-watchers to run the half mile to a street where a window-cleaning friend had a ladder which he had agreed to let them use. By the time they had staggered back with it to Wilmer Road, any building that had caught fire would have burnt down. Before the end of the war, the window-cleaner and his friend quarrelled and the use of the ladder was withdrawn! St Agatha however remained popular and proved a truer friend than the window-cleaner as the parish of St Cuthbert's, its priests and parishioners, ended the war without even so much as a scratch.

Spring 1940 saw Father O'Connor, in spite of the war, busy with speaking engagements at conferences and summer schools. In June he took a group of young people to a summer school in Cambridge where they witnessed 200 aliens being rounded up. The encounter led to an unexpected bonus for two young girls in his party who spotted two nuns with very hairy arms and wearing wrist watches. Drawing the attention of the police to the hairy nuns resulted in the girls being rewarded with the substantial sum of fifty shillings.

Back in his own parish Father O'Connor led a retreat, during the course of which he gave five talks before giving another at the Bar Convent in York. He went on to give a third retreat to Mother Kevin's novices at Holme Hall where she had started a Uganda noviciate in 1928 to train missionaries for East Africa. The following week he was preaching at the Silver Jubilee of Mother Emmanuel, his new friend at Holme Hall. Mother Kevin herself was well known to him as her work received generous support every year from St Bede's school. Returned from Africa, she died in 1957, in the Franciscan Missionary Sisters for Africa convent in Boston, USA.

In early 1940, Father O'Connor wrote two articles for *The Downside Review* both entitled 'Some Footnotes to the Life of Père Lamy' from Maurice Berthon's *Three Months with Père Lamy*. He was quite immersed in the life of Jean Edouard Lamy at the time as he was translating, from the French, Comte Paul Biver's biography of this twentieth-century visionary priest. He was widely known as the rag pickers' priest for his championing of the poor orphan boys in his parish who scratched a living by collecting rags. He prayed the rosary

almost continually as a vision of the Blessed Virgin had shown
Père Lamy the great power of this prayer to reach the heart of
God and overcome the Devil, sentiments with which Father
O'Connor, with his own love of the rosary, would agree.

Father O'Connor had a parishioner who was a very good
typist and who had the use of a typewriter in the evenings due
to the war! The lady was a secretary in the town and her boss
wished her to take charge of the typewriter in case the office
was bombed and the typewriter destroyed. This proved very
convenient for Father O'Connor, if not for the lady herself, as
he needed someone to type up his translation of the book and
persuaded her to take on the job.

Towards the end of 1940, Dame Werburg sent Father
O'Connor a picture of her wood engraving entitled *I Am the
Ground of Thy Beseeching,* words from the last chapter of
Sixteen Revelations of Divine Love, by Julian of Norwich.
Published towards the end of the fourteenth century, the book
details the series of intense visions experienced during a severe
illness. Father O'Connor was thrilled that Dame Werburg was
taking notice of Mother Juliana, who was such a dear, and
ordered a gross of the engravings for a friend's ordination. He
liked to read a chapter of the *Revelations of Divine Love,* edited
by Roger Hudleston the Downside Abbey monk, last thing
almost every night.

In January 1941, Father O'Connor requested Dame Werburg
to send him a dozen or two prayer cards bearing an engraving
entitled *The Praying Christ.* He promised immediate payment
for the cards which he intended to give to parishioners who
only attended Mass sporadically. The engraving had been
commissioned by Abbé Paul Couturier for his Christian Unity
movement and the printed prayer cards appeared in English,
French, German and Latin versions. The prayer card appeared
in *Sobornost*, the journal of the Fellowship of St Alban and St
Sergius whose aim was to build up the relationship between
eastern and western Christians.

Some versions of the prayer card had English or French
prayers or meditations on the reverse and a couple of months
after receiving his consignment, Father O'Connor told Dame

Werburg that he was going to compose his own meditation on *The Praying Christ*. This was subsequently printed by the Stanbrook Abbey Press and in 1964, they produced a special edition on Japanese Natsumé paper. Father O'Connor would have been delighted with it.

Father O'Connor continued to give many minor commissions to Dame Werburg during the 1940s but in 1950 they collaborated on *The Way of the Cross*. The booklet was illustrated with photographs of Dame Werburg's paintings, in oil on wood, of the Stations of the Cross for the Church of Christ the King, Bromborough in Cheshire, with meditations written to accompany them by Father O'Connor. The booklet was produced by the Stanbrook Abbey Press in two slightly differing versions.

During the war, when she wasn't carving, weaving, painting and not forgetting taking part in her religious duties, Dame Werburg took over the running of the Abbey orchard. She kept Father O'Connor up to date with accounts of her success, or lack of it, and he, as always, was on hand to offer advice. She seems to have been having trouble with some kind of insects or grubs on her apples as he suggests she hang a wide-mouthed jar of water on every branch at the end of May or early June and observe what happens during the summer nights. Unfortunately, none of the surviving letters tell us what happened, presumably something fell in the water and drowned thus solving the problem. Dame Werburg herself had a nasty fall from the apple tree, happily not into water, as she climbed her ladder to collect the fruit. Father O'Connor was sympathetic but advised her that, after concussion, she should avoid whisky and strong wines, however difficult that might be for her!

Dame Werburg also worked in the vegetable garden where she was having trouble producing a good crop of onions. Father O'Connor lost no time in telling her she needed to induce the chaplain to bless a pan of holy water and sprinkle this around the vegetable plot, a method that had produced a fine of crop of turnips back home in Ireland. What it did for onions we are left to surmise. With food being so scarce during wartime, one summer when Bradford market had a glut of onions, Father O'Connor considered it worth mentioning the fact in his next letter to the gardening nun. Dame Werburg's artistic abilities have been recognized but she was certainly doing her bit for the war effort with her manual labours.

On Friday 7 July 1944, a service of Benediction was broadcast by the BBC at which Father O'Connor gave the Address. In it he spoke of the respect shown for Friday, the day Our Lord suffered and died for us, and especially for the first Friday of each month, which, as had been revealed by the Lord to a seventeenth-century French nun, would receive special reward. It was a day to receive Holy Communion and spend time in contemplation before the Blessed Sacrament. Though it was easy to see and think of the physical suffering the human body of Our Lord endured, Father O'Connor suggested his listeners think how the human mind of Our Lord also suffered as he contemplated all the sins and possible offences against God. Father O'Connor felt he was daring to suggest that Our Lord was suffering the pain of loss, the eternal consequence of the dreadful world of evil.

The following year, to celebrate his fifty years as a priest, Father O'Connor, ably assisted by the senior pupils of St Joseph's, sang a High Mass of Thanksgiving at St Cuthbert's church on 3 April 1945. The Gregorian plainsong, *Missa Lux et Origo*, was an appropriate choice for this Easter Tuesday. The Right Revd Henry Poskitt, Bishop of Leeds, presided and the church was filled with diocesan clergy, friends and parishioners. Father O'Connor was presented with an illuminated address and a cheque for £1,340 by his friends and parishioners, the latter no doubt grateful that, not only had he built them a new church, but the heavy debt on the old one had been discharged.

Father O'Connor hoped to retire after his Golden Jubilee and suggested to the bishop that he be allowed to live on in the presbytery, but with his curate replacing him as parish priest. The bishop rejected this suggestion and Father O'Connor remained parish priest until his death but his workload was eased, when two curates, Fathers Keegan and Maudsley, replaced Father Casey the following year.

In November, Father O'Connor sent a watercolour by David Cox of St Edmund's Abbey, Bury St Edmunds, to Douai Abbey, also dedicated to St Edmund. Father Ignatius Rice was to use the picture as he deemed fit, if necessary he was free to sell it to supply funds for anything that might be to the good of the school. Dom Ignatius deemed it best to keep the picture at Douai, where it resides to the present day. Father O'Connor lived for almost another seven years after his Golden Jubilee but he began assessing his art collection, further donations followed, valuations were sought and a London sale was later arranged.

In January 1946 Father O'Connor wrote to the London art dealers, Spink and Son; unfortunately there is only their reply among Father O'Connor's papers in the John Kelly Library. They acknowledged that Father O'Connor was sending them a Teniers picture, and a Da Vinci drawing by registered post and a framed Turner and another Da Vinci, *Head of a Boy*, by rail and that after careful study they would report back to him, presumably concerning authenticity and value. In the auction held in Bradford after his death, there was a picture on copper entitled *St Anthony in the Desert,* by David Teniers, Senior, and a number of paintings by J. M. W. Turner, which may have been among those sent to London. Of the Da Vinci drawings there is no further mention in either the 1952 sale or a previous sale at Christie's, so they may have been sold through Spink and Son at the time. It would have been interesting to know if Father O'Connor had indeed owned two Leonardo da Vinci drawings, and the value of them, but, as Spinks no longer hold records for that period, they were unable to shed any light on the matter.

Later the same year, Father O'Connor donated a portrait of St John Baptist de la Salle as Canon of Rheims to Douai Abbey. Father O'Connor was sure of the identity of the sitter as he and his school friends in Flanders had each received a picture of him when they assisted at his beatification ceremony in 1889. Though the artist was unknown, Father O'Connor assured Dom Ignatius that it was a highly penetrating likeness, and the saint's squint, while still there, was beautifully treated. Father

O'Connor had bought the painting after discovering it in a Bradford furniture warehouse where he had also discovered a painting by the fifteenth-century Italian artist, Il Pintoricchio. He was alone in his conviction that this was a genuine Pintoricchio but he was again proved correct as *The Holy Family with the Infant Saint John, in a landscape* was duly sold at Christie's for ninety-five guineas.

Yet another donation to Douai by Father O'Connor was a portrait of an unknown man wearing clerical garb and holding what appears to be a bible in his right hand. Father O'Connor wondered if the portrait could be by Philippe de Champaigne, though he supposed it to be 'too quiet for him'.[7] Father O'Connor was right, it wasn't by this artist and further investigation by Father Leo Arkwright of Douai in 1973 failed to discover who the artist was but it was sold at auction in 1989 by Sotheby's in London.

In 1946, Blackfriars published a small work on Jerome Savonarola by Father O'Connor. Ambrose Farrell, reviewing it for *Blackfriars* journal in August 1947, wrote it off as merely a collection of rough notes which provided a provocative sketch of Savonarola' s career. Though G. K. Chesterton had included Savonarola in his *Twelve Types*, published in 1902, Father O'Connor had long tried to persuade him to write a book on the subject, as had his publishers, but Frances thought Gilbert just had so many other things to do that he would not get round to it for a long time. Of course he never did get round to it, and Father O'Connor's short work didn't make up for it.

Among Father O'Connor's papers in the John Kelly Library is an intriguing letter from R. H. Spurr art dealers and valuers, dated November 1949. The content of this letter suggests he was being consulted about a particular work of art. Unfortunately, the work isn't named, but R. H. Spurr was very impressed by it, one of the finest works of its type he had handled, he said, and he felt that Father O'Connor should see it. Accordingly he was coming from Southport on the west coast of Lancashire, to Bradford so the priest could see it for himself and have a chat about it. He ends the letter 'If it was of little or no importance I would not have troubled the owner or you as I am doing.' It all sounds a little unusual, but R. H. Spurr had owned the Romney Galleries in Bradford before moving to Southport and no doubt had had previous dealings with Father O'Connor and was aware of his reputation in the world of art.

Notes

1. Benedictines of Stanbrook Abbey, *In A Great Tradition*.
2. *L' Artisan Liturgique*, p. 1079.
3. O'Connor, *Letter*, 3 October 1936, Stanbrook Abbey.
4. *L' Artisan Liturgique,* p. 1111.
5. O'Connor, *Why Revive the Liturgy and How?* p. 11.
6. *House Chronicle*, 2–3 May 1939, Stanbrook Abbey.
7. O'Connor, *Letter*, 3 July 1946, Douai Abbey.

Chapter 13

1950–2: Goodbye to Father Brown

Early in 1950, Father O'Connor was praying at Mass for 'Barney' Shaw, whose health was then causing concern, but confessed to Dame Werburg that he himself was 'getting more interested in the other world than this, great and jolly as I find this one'.[1] He began to plan for the disposal of his worldly goods, as he wanted his cousin, Miss Dorothy Duggan, to benefit from his expensive habit of acquiring pictures and chinoiserie and had been advised by his accountants to sell up. Consequently, the auctioneers Christie & Co were called in, but only forty-six paintings and drawings from his collection were put up for auction on 28 July 1950. These included drawings by Cotman, Millais and Niemann with the highest prices of twenty and twenty-four guineas being given for *The Adoration of the Magi* by Brueghel and *Desolation* by Apol respectively. The highest price paid for a painting was 230 guineas for an early Italian *Madonna and Child* by Francesco Francia. As might be expected there were a number of paintings of religious subjects but there were a few still life paintings, landscapes and portraits, the latter including one each by Della Francesca and Anthony Van Dyck. This auction raised a total 1,593 guineas and there was plenty left to auction another day. Asked about Father O'Connor's art collection, Father Keegan, one of the two curates at this time, didn't think there was anything of great value among the pictures cluttering up the presbytery as they had often been picked up in small shops with names such as 'Treasures and Bygones'. Father O'Connor had the ability to know which were the genuine treasures, and the artists represented in his collection were of national and international repute, but his curates were probably so used to him arriving home with his brown paper parcels that they never gave a thought to what they actually contained.

A number of letters among Father O'Connor's papers in the John Kelly Library concern a painting he had given to his cousin in 1923. The first letter, dated 2 May 1928, is from the Dutch artist Nico Jungman acknowledging receipt of his own picture, *Madonna and Child*. Father O'Connor had sent the picture to the artist, who lived and worked in London, to have some restoration work done on it. On 3 October three years later, the artist wrote to say that he was sorry that he hadn't had time to do anything to the panel but hoped to start work on it in the immediate future. The *Madonna* was still in his studio when he died in 1935 as correspondence between Nico's daughter, Zita, and Miss Duggan show. Judging by Zita's replies, it appears that Miss Duggan had written to her enquiring about the picture as Zita says she has a parcel with 'Belonging to the Bradford priest' written on the outside. The parcel contained a tempera panel, approx 16ins x 14ins, of a Madonna and Child painted by her father which matched Miss Duggan's description. As it was the only picture left unaccounted for after her father's death, Zita was very happy to have found the owner. The picture finally arrived back at St Cuthbert's presbytery in May 1936, presumably in the same condition that it left.

Father O'Connor sent his portrait of G. K. Chesterton by James Gunn, to Dorothy Collins, along with other Chesterton items, for an agreed sum to be paid to his cousin rather than sending them to auction. He had bought the crayon drawing in 1933 from E.W. Hudson who was having to sell it, along with many other possessions including his London house, after being made redundant. Hudson had bought it after seeing it in a recent exhibition of Gunn's work at the Barbison House galleries. The asking price was twenty pounds but when it was still unsold at the close of the exhibition, he had acquired it for ten guineas, the sum for which Father O'Connor bought it from him.

The other items sent to Miss Collins included autographed books, and Chesterton's own and others' letters on his conversion. On the back of one of them is a pencilled note that the letters were bought for ten pounds from Father O'Connor and that they could be reproduced. In this letter Father O'Connor added that he hoped to visit Dorothy in December 'if God spares me. It seems to be a habit with him'.[2]

Although he was disposing of some of his worldly goods and was feeling that his days in this world were numbered, Father O'Connor was still to be seen at local cultural events. On 1 July 1950, it was noted in the local newspaper that, looking as youthful as ever, he was amongst the well-known Bradfordians present at the opening of an exhibition of work by William Rothenstein which was opened by his son, John Rothenstein, then Director of the Tate Gallery in London.

John Rothenstein recalled how his late father, in his fifteen years as principal of the Royal College of Art, had always a particular affection for his Yorkshire students. Born close by the Cartwright Hall Gallery where the exhibition was held, Yorkshire had always exercised an extraordinary influence on William Rothenstein's art from the beginning to the end. His son wondered whether Yorkshire folk realized how prominent the county was in the production of artists. 'No' would seem to be the appropriate answer to that. In his speech the Lord Mayor admitted that he was not a connoisseur of art; he had tried looking at so-called 'modern art' from a distance and from close to but his sense of art didn't seem to respond. Both William Rothenstein and Father O'Connor had come across this lack of response during their years of involvement with the gallery while I described William as 'The Forgotten Son of Bradford' in an article for the *Yorkshire Journal*. Local artists are now treated rather better; David Hockney who was born in Bradford and attended the local art college in the city, has a whole gallery dedicated to his work, and is a frequent and well-known visitor to the city.

George Bernard Shaw had managed to hold on to life for almost the whole of 1950 but died, aged ninety-four, on 2 November. The following month Father O'Connor celebrated his eightieth birthday with a magnificent cake topped by a model of St Cuthbert's church.

In 1951, Father O'Connor made the first major changes to the style of St Cuthbert's church. In an attempt to simplify the facilities for worship, the reredos was removed and replaced with a draped backcloth in front of which was a crucifix, while the altar was replaced with one of a more simple design. It seems that Father O'Connor may have planned at least one change just prior to the outbreak of war in 1939.

In a letter to Dame Werburg he said that he would send her 'a photograph of the window if and when'.[3] No further mention of this was ever made so it appeared that it was more a case of if than of when, but among Father O'Connor's papers in the John Kelly Library, there is an invitation from Leonard Walker to the viewing of an east window for St Cuthbert's church together with a number of watercolours. The exhibition was to be held 12–18 February at the artist's London studio. The envelope, with a 1940 postmark, had originally been addressed to Mr F. L. Pollack, in Park Court, Bradford, a friend and parishioner of Father O'Connor to whom the envelope had been re-addressed. This suggests that Frederick Leo Pollack was about to finance a new window for the church. The curator at The Stained Glass Museum was unable to confirm whether or not the window was ever made, and as there is no record of it ever appearing at the church, it seems the project never got beyond the design stage. This is not surprising considering there was a war on and, with bombs being dropped all over the country, it was hardly the time for commissioning new windows by renowned stained glass artists.

Father O'Connor's letters, never the easiest to read, become even more difficult in the early part of 1951. He was having massage for rheumatism, spending the day in his dressing gown and writing letters balanced on his knee. He thought all letters should be written in Lent as they were a penance, but this was most likely due to his failing health as it is doubtful he felt the

many letters he wrote throughout his busy life to be a
punishment. He had enjoyed Dame Werburg's letter in
January; it had been the best of all the season's greetings,
however he thought her a bit too laconic for a true
contemplative! His last letter to Dame Werburg was written in
June 1951, shortly after he had ceased to take an active part in
parochial work, and thought that 'even if they held me back
from heaven they might come for me in a rush'. They didn't
and, after a short stay in the Duke of York's Nursing Home in
Bradford, he was moved to the Sisters of Mercy Nursing
Home, St Joseph's in Horsforth, near Leeds, later in the year.

A photograph in a national newspaper showed Father
O'Connor smoking a pipe in bed at the nursing home on his
eighty-first birthday. A beaten brass bowl, holding two other
favourite pipes, lay on his bedside table together with a bible
and a copy of *The People's Priest,* by the then Bishop of Leeds,
Dr J. C. Heenan. Frail in body as Father O'Connor now was,
his mind remained active and he left as lasting an impression at
the nursing home as he did anywhere. What that impression
was I heard from the twenty-two-year-old nurse who had been
assigned to his care.

Gabrielle had considered it a privilege to be his nurse, so
much so that she stayed at the nursing home twenty-four hours
a day to be near him. She had stayed the first time as Father
O'Connor was worried about her having difficulty getting
home in the snow, so a bed had been found for her at the
nursing home. After that first night, she never spent another
away until after his death many months later. As Father
O'Connor required more attention than the nuns were able to
give him, and Gabrielle needed to get away from a difficult
situation in Wakefield, her wise parish priest suggested she
move to Horsforth where they might help each other. His
suggestion was acted upon and an affinity between the patient
and the nurse he always referred to as 'child' became apparent
at once.

Father O'Connor, though not completely bedridden, was
confined to his room so he made a small altar where he was
able to say Mass until he became too weak. He would never

have flowers on it after he had once seen an earwig close to the Sacred Host and wasn't taking any chances. While acknowledging that God is always present during the sacrifice of the Mass, when Father O'Connor said Mass, his nurse had the strong feeling that at the Transubstantiation 'God had opened the door and come in.' God was truly Father O'Connor's great friend, she recalled, someone he would talk about as though they had just enjoyed a round of golf together. This in no way made him 'holier than thou' however, quite the reverse in fact, as he had not mellowed with old age and could still be very abrupt.

As God was his friend, a real and powerful enemy was the Devil, and Father O'Connor talked about him at length. Nurse Gabrielle remembered him telling her a story about the chaplain of a large mental hospital who, if he was carrying the Blessed Sacrament as he passed through the common room, was always attacked by one of the patients, even though the Sacrament was not in view. If the priest didn't have the Sacrament about him, the patient would leave him alone. On a lighter note, Father O'Connor had once asked the boys in his Sunday school if they knew how to 'raise the devil'. He answered his own question by telling them to 'put the cat through the mangle'! Of course the devil Father O'Connor was speaking about was the angry mother, who would no doubt have had something sharp to say about her parish priest putting such an outrageous idea into her child's head.

Father O'Connor was still able to remember and recite reams of poetry, and often his visitors would be called upon to recite a poem for him. As his interest in ghost stories had not waned, they might instead be asked to supply such a story. Rather more visitors were able to supply a poem than a ghostly tale, but one person was able to tell him of a personal encounter with the ghost of someone very close to her. After telling him exactly what had happened, she was comforted by Father O'Connor's explanation of the occurrence, of how God occasionally allowed a deceased loved one to come to the aid of a person in distress.

In return for this story, Father O'Connor told her one of his own about a priest who had been called out one night by a woman who led him the short distance to a block of palatial apartments. After ringing the doorbell of one of them, the woman left him. A hale and hearty middle-aged man answered the door and invited the priest into the beautiful flat. In answer to his query, the man assured him he was there alone, there was no invalid or sick person in the house. As the priest walked out of the room he caught sight of a photograph of the woman who had brought him and was told she was the man's mother who had died six years previously. This obviously shook the priest but it shocked the man into going to confession the next morning, shortly after which he was found dead in bed. Readers' may draw their own conclusions but this story is typical of a number of instances Father O'Connor collected of ghosts appearing in order to right a wrong.

Even when surrounded by competent nursing staff, Father O'Connor didn't hesitate to apply his own methods of healing when he thought it necessary. When one of the nurses became sick herself and confined to bed with a very high temperature, shivering and streaming with cold, he poured a glass of gin from his own bottle, blessed it and sent it to her, saying she should drink it with some hot water. She could only manage three mouthfuls of the 'holy spirit' but it proved very effective for she was back on duty next morning completely restored. More seriously, his own powers of healing seemed not to have diminished for it is reported that he halted the rapid deterioration of the eyes of a young child in the nursing home who was going blind.

On the morning of 6 Feb 1952, the day of Father O'Connor's death, his nurse was slightly taken aback when she went into his room and he said that the King had stolen a march on him. Not realising what he meant, she later heard that King George VI had died, suggesting that Father O'Connor knew he himself was now close to death. Another version of this story is that what he actually said was 'the old bugger's beaten me' which does indeed sound more his style. During the afternoon, however, he was well enough for a discussion on higher education with a friend but later had a sudden collapse and received the Last Rites from Father Donovan, a fellow patient. Gabrielle stayed by his bedside, holding his hand as they prayed the rosary together. As she watched him slip peacefully away, she had the feeling she had nursed a saint. An Anglican doctor and close friend of Father O'Connor was similarly moved and was heard to remark that they had lost a saint that day. Later a patient who moved into his room at the nursing home felt it held such a sense of complete and utter peace that the previous occupant, of whom she had no knowledge, must have been a very spiritual person. Indeed a friend seeing the look of peace and joy and the stamp of holiness on Father O'Connor's face as he lay in his coffin, had the impression he was saying 'There I told you what it would be like, and now I know what it is to see God.'

The Requiem Mass for Mgr John Joseph O'Connor was held in St Cuthbert's, the church he had served as parish priest for thirty-two years. The Mass was sung by his long-standing friend Dom Ignatius Rice, with more than 150 clergy chanting the liturgical music, led by Bishop Heenan. In the centre aisle the coffin bore Mgr O'Connor's golden chalice and biretta. He had few surviving relatives, just two cousins and a nephew represented the family but there was no lack of mourners. They came from every walk of life: the Lord Mayor of Bradford, the Head Postmaster, the Matron of Bradford Royal Infirmary, representatives from the business world, from the arts, from education, representatives from every major committee in the city, parishioners, schoolchildren and teachers. Men wearing business suits or boiler suits, women in fur coats or shawls, knelt side-by-side, as they paid their last respects to the man who had regarded them all as friends. Mgr O'Connor, Father O'Connor, Father John or just Johnny, by whatever name he was addressed, he was, the bishop said, 'an essentially simple man', unique and not a typical parish priest, but 'nevertheless like all great characters, he was sometimes the cause of bewilderment to those who did not know him'. So many who thought they knew him, in reality, barely knew him at all.

Mgr O'Connor, clothed in a purple 'Ditchling' vestment, was buried at Scholemoor Cemetery, Bradford on a cold, blustery day with sunshine and snow showers. His funeral, on 11 February, took place as the body of King George VI travelled from Sandringham to London where it would lie in state. His daughter, Princess Elizabeth when she left England, was on her way home from South Africa as Queen Elizabeth II. The end of an era, it seems typical of Father O'Connor to have left this world in such good company.

Father O'Connor's death was widely reported in national and local newspapers, carrying headlines such as *Father Brown's case book closes*; *G. K. Chesterton's 'Father Brown' dies*; *Many-sided 'Fr Brown'*. His obituary in *The Douai Magazine* [4] recalled his affection for anything or anyone connected with Douai. He attended as many gatherings of Dowegians as possible and was invariably the life and soul of the party but his great love of the Mass and the liturgy was evident to all and his love of good company was founded on St Paul's injunction to be 'all things to all men'.

S. M. Albert, writing in *Blackfriars,* [5] gives a glimpse of how Father O'Connor was regarded by the Dominican Order to whom he had been an old and staunch friend but, although he had been a great admirer of the Order, he had been too much of a free-lance to become a tertiary. Albert considered Father O'Connor to be both a true Dominican and Thomist at heart. Dominican too was his love of the rosary and he established the Rosary Confraternity in his church. He enjoyed leading the October devotions before the Lady Altar, kneeling in the front bench and, after the rosary had been recited, turning round to present his deep thoughts on its mysteries to those gathered with him. The roses blessed on Rosary Sunday were not distributed to the congregation as was usual, but were presented by the children for later distribution to the sick (cleverly combining three of his great loves, of the rosary, of children and of the sick).

With Father O'Connor peacefully laid to rest, the business of sorting out and disposing of his vast accumulation of art and artefacts, books, bits and bobs, began in earnest. Father O'Connor left no will, having given freely throughout his life to his churches, parishioners and friends and making it known that his cousin Dorothy was to benefit from the proceeds of the sale of his goods. Father Kevin Scannell, parish priest at St Mary's church, Horsforth, was a constant visitor to Father O'Connor's bedside and no doubt discussed with him the great love they shared for G. K. Chesterton but it was about Eric Gill's work that Dorothy Duggan wrote to him some months after Father O'Connor's death.

Miss Duggan was in Bradford helping to organize the auction sale that would take place in December and considered, as did a number of others, that certain items by Gill should not go to the saleroom but be sold privately. These included copies of *The Song of Songs,* containing Gill's illustrations, and an assorted number of prints together with some of the first Ditchling publications. Miss Duggan thought Father Scannell might know someone who would appreciate these items which she didn't want to 'get into the wrong hands – as these things are only really for the "Few"'. No doubt she felt that some of the items left behind would have shocked Father O'Connor's parishioners unaware of the extent of his commitment to Gill and his work.

The Bradford auction by Ernest R. de Rome took place over two days in December, and attracted dealers from London as well as St Cuthbert parishioners hoping to buy themselves some small reminder of their unique parish priest. The first one hundred lots to go under the hammer were Chinese pottery and porcelain, thirty-two of them being sold for £116 in the first half-hour. Next came twenty carved ivories, some of which must have been carved by Dame Werburg but no artists' names were given. Fourteen Italian, classical and other bronzes, including a Gill nude of a seated Mother with suckling Child, were followed by a further twenty-nine Chinese bronze bowls, vases, jardinières, incense burners and a Buddha. The final twenty-seven lots of the day were a miscellaneous collection of Staffordshire pottery figures, carved wooden figures, marble panels, blue and white Delft pieces, brass candlesticks and yet another jardinière, not to mention an Imari vase, a majolica fish and a number of ashtrays. The first day ended having raised approximately £1,000.

The second day's sale was of books and yet more pictures,

over nine hundred of the former and one hundred and seven of the latter. Father O'Connor's wide interests were well represented by his books, poetry, Shakespeare, Greek drama and Irish history, Catholic literature, travel, painting and books on collecting bronzes, Chinese vases, and Sheffield plate. Of course many of the books were written by his friends: Chesterton, Belloc, Shaw, Max Beerbohm and Compton Mackenzie, while many of these were autographed first editions or limited editions. Few of Father O'Connor's parishioners would be aware of the excitement being generated around the world by this sale and how many of the items would come to rest in American and Canadian universities.

The bidding for *The Secret of Father Brown,* in a highly coloured paper jacket, started quietly but developed into a duel between two would-be buyers, Father Scannell and an un-named buyer who successfully acquired the book for forty pounds. On the flyleaf was an inscription to Father O'Connor from Chesterton, while on the endpaper he had written a parody of a folk song beginning 'Six detectives went fishing' which was based on a favourite folk song that Father O'Connor often performed at his friend's request, beginning 'Six Dukes they went fishing'. The song was also performed by George Maxwell at the annual gathering of the Guild of St Joseph and St Dominic. The book was bought by 'Paul' from Leeds who had remained anonymous lest his wife be upset, but later he gave the book to Father Scannell and it is now in the John Kelly Library, the University of St Michael's College, Toronto.

Father Scannell made a successful bid of twenty-two pounds for *The Ball and the Cross,* with its holograph poem on Heckmondwike. His brother (Father Patrick F. Scannell) had attended the auction in order to keep Father Kevin from losing his head, but found himself stepping in, when Kevin stopped bidding, to buy *The Ballad of the White Horse* for twenty pounds. Patrick also gave the book, which contained a holograph of the second poem about Heckmondwike, to his brother at a later date. This too is now in the John Kelly Library.

The nearest Father Scannell ever got to G. K. Chesterton

was hearing him lecture in Bradford. As a curate at St Joseph's, Bradford, during the Depression of the 1930s, he saw the effect this was having on the parishioners, and was very impressed by Chesterton's writings on these things, recognizing a born Catholic and humanitarian. He began to build up a priceless collection of Chestertoniana including the original manuscript of *The Surprise,* a rare copy of the pantomime *The Turkey and the Turk,* obtained page by page from colleagues of the printer which he then had bound, and a copy of *The Legend of the Sword* tracked down in Dublin.

One of the book dealers who attended the auction of Father O'Connor's books came from Lancashire and more than a hundred of the books he bought in Bradford appeared the following year in his sale of 'Rare and Important Books'. These included presentation copies of works by both Chesterton and Belloc. Two books by Belloc, *On Anything,* and *Verses,* found their last resting place in Boston College, Massachusetts, the *Verses* having come via this Southport bookseller.

In 1953, Father Scannell received a letter from John Bennett Shaw of Tulsa, Oklahoma, thanking him for the full report of the O'Connor sale and a number of gifts including copies of the three Chesterton poetic inscriptions. Father Scannell regarded the collector as one of the 'Few' to be trusted with a list of the items from Father O'Connor's collection of Gill and Ditchling material and sent this on to him. In his letter, Shaw had noted those items he would like to purchase and the prices he was prepared to offer for them, in spite of a setback in his oil business when his latest drilling produced only a dry hole.

John Bennett Shaw was particularly anxious to acquire *The Passion of Perpetua and Felicity* as he had missed several chances during the last twenty years to acquire it. For this he was offering fifteen dollars, more than he thought it was probably worth but he would pay it anyway. An unbound, uncut edition of *The Song of the Soul* was worth three dollars fifty to him as he already had a copy but was he quite keen to learn bookbinding. Among his remaining requests was Father O'Connor's translation of *The Philosophy of Art* which he currently valued at seven dollars fifty. Father Scannell duly dispatched the seven chosen items to Tulsa with a note that twenty dollars, rather than the thirty-six dollars list price, would be acceptable. He requested, however, that Shaw should not send the money but keep it to pay eventually for the Chesterton material Father Scannell was hoping he would be able to locate for him in America. The Gill items purchased by Shaw were probably among the collection he later donated to his Alma Mater, the University of Notre Dame, Indiana.

At the beginning of 1954, Father Scannell sent the list of Father O'Connor' s Gill collection to another one of the 'Few', in this case Eric Gill's own brother Evan who was Liverpool's Town Clerk. After making a valuation of the publications and engravings, he wrote to Father Scannell suggesting a total of just over £141, plus drawings and prints not yet priced. He said he had made the prices low compared with those asked by a dealer as, in the majority of cases, they were still to be circulated among a select group of friends, including other Gill siblings. Evan was proposing, however, sending some items to the University of California to be held in perpetuity. He also intended contacting two, un-named, collectors in America.

Cecil Gill and John Bennett Shaw were in competition for a David Jones *Nude* and two of his copper engravings. According to Evan Gill, Shaw had offered twenty-five dollars for the former and seven dollars fifty for the latter but they went to Cecil with his higher bid of ten pounds and three pounds respectively. If Father Scannell approved, Evan planned to double the price offered by Shaw for three of Eric's drawings from eight to fifteen dollars each, which Evan still thought to be very, very cheap, but he would like Shaw to have them as he was in 'another category' and they would be going to a good home. These three drawings were of two nudes, signed, dated and with a greeting to Father O'Connor; a nude torso, similarly signed and with a greeting; and a drawing of the proposed altar for Father O'Connor's Church of First Martyrs. He would also offer Shaw a further three prints of woodcuts by Desmond Chute and David Jones, together with thirty-seven proofs of Eric's wood engravings. Evan Gill also sought Father Scannell's approval for offering a St Dominic's Press book of

Wood-Engravings to his un-named friend in America for twelve pounds. Shaw had offered fifteen to twenty dollars but as his friend was keen to have the book, and again had posterity in mind for his collection, he hoped Father Scannell would agree.

After his death, Evan Gill wanted his own collection of books, drawings, prints and manuscripts relating to Ditchling and its historical role in art and craft, and centred around Eric, to remain intact. It was bought by a dealer in the 1960s who preserved it largely untouched for forty years before it was agreed, in 2004, to offer the Ditchling Museum the opportunity to buy it for £110,000. It took two years to raise the money, with the help of the Heritage Lottery fund and various other grants and donations, and the collection was finally acquired in May 2006 and has now been made available to researchers by appointment. Not all the items on Evan Gill's list crossed the Atlantic; copies of Eric's *Art and Love* and *Art and Prudence,* published by the Golden Cockerel Press, have come to rest at Ditching and there may be more when a full check has been carried out. Both these books have inscriptions to Father O'Connor, *Art and Prudence* being dedicated 'To the Revd John O'Connor, in whose house this essay was written, from his most devoted and affectionate, Eric G.' *Art and Love* also contains a letter.

Father Scannell lectured on Chesterton, and his Father Brown, both locally and in America and considered there to be a much greater interest on the other side of the Atlantic. Which, indeed, still seems to be the case. However, there were many letters of condemnation in the Yorkshire newspapers (in Father O'Connor's papers in the John Kelly Library) when it was discovered that Father Scannell's collection, together with Father O'Connor's own archival material, was to be bequeathed to the Pontifical Institute of Medieval Studies, University of St Michael's College, Toronto, Canada. When Father Scannell died aged seventy-four in July 1976, the collection was duly dispatched. It was later transferred to the Rare Books division of the John Kelly Library at St Michael's where it forms the basis of their Chesterton collection.

Though many of his material goods have found homes

Fr O'Connor's grave in Scholemoor Cemetery, Bradford.

hundreds, even thousands of miles away from Yorkshire, Father O'Connor's legacy lives on in bricks and mortar in Heckmondwike and Bradford. But despite his national and international reputation as an intellectual, it is as a caring, compassionate, occasionally irascible, parish priest that he is fondly remembered, over fifty years after his death, by his ex-parishioners. Sadly, many of those interviewed have now themselves died without ever knowing all that their beloved priest got up to during his absences from his parish.

I was asked when writing the book if I thought I would have liked Father O'Connor had I known him. Occasionally, I have had to remind myself that I hadn't known him as I felt I had become so close to him during the writing of this biography, so I had no hesitation in replying, 'Yes, I think I would.' At the end of his story, I hope my readers feel they too would have enjoyed meeting *The Elusive Father Brown*.

Notes

1. O'Connor, Letter,14 July 1950, Stanbrook Abbey.
2. O'Connor, *Letter*, 9 August 1950, British Library.
3. O'Connor, *Letter*, 13 March 1939, Stanbrook Abbey.
4. 'Right Rev. Mgr. J. O'Connor', *The Douai Magazine*, pp. 58–9.
5. Albert, 'John O'Connor', *Blackfriars*, pp. 213–8.

Appendix I

Publications of Father O'Connor, books, articles, translations, book reviews by year of publication.

1897   *The Douai Magazine*, 'The Landing of St Augustine', vol. xi, May.

1898   *Arundel Hymns*, edited by Henry Duke of Norfolk & C. T. Gatty (Boosey & Co., London & New York), contributor.

1908   Crashaw, Richard, *A Plea for April Showers*, translation.

1913   *The Weld Sermon* (Downside Abbey, Bath).

1918   Thompson, F., *Mistress of Vision*, commentary.

1922   *The Sower*, 'A few remarks about the relation of children with the Blessed Sacrament', no. 40, September.
       The Douai Magazine, 'St Alban', vol. 2, no. 2, July.
       The Venerabile, 'The First Meeting of the Roman Association at Rome', vol.1, no.1, October.

1923   *The Hindley Children's Mass*, music by Dom Alphege Shebbeare (G. F. Sewell, Bradford).
       Maritain, Jacques, *The Philosophy of Art* (St Dominic's Press, Ditchling), translation.
       The Venerabile, 'Spontaneities', vol. 1, no. 3, October.

1925   *The Song of Songs* (Golden Cockerel Press, Waltham St Lawrence), engravings by Eric Gill, text edited and amended by Fr O'Connor.

1926   *The Venerabile*, 'Monsignor John Prior', vol. III, no.1, October.
       The Douai Magazine, 'A Fit of Anecdotage', vol. IV, no. 2.

1927   *The Song of the Soul* (Francis Walterson, Capel-y-ffin), engravings by Eric Gill, translation.
1928   *Why Revive the Liturgy & How?* (Private circulation).
1928   *Blackfriars*, 'Lauda Sion', June.
       The Sower, 'The Infancy of Fr Brown', no. 88, July.
1929   *Blackfriars*, Book review of *The Mysteriousness of Marriage*, March.
       Blackfriars, 'After the Elevation', words to Schubert's music no.70 in *Arundel Hymns*, March.
       Blackfriars, 'A Note on Dante's *Paradiso*', July.
       Blackfriars, 'St Dominic' (translation of St Dominic's Sequence in the Dominican Missal), August.
1930   *Blackfriars*, Richard Crashaw, 'Yoke of Oxen', translation, May.
       Blackfriars, Two carols from *Two Hundred Folk Carols*, December.
       Blackfriars, 'Ironic & Socratic', review of Plato's *Britannia*, by Douglas Woodruff, December.
       Bookman, 'Eric Gill: Searcher for Reality', December.
1931   Claudel, Paul, *The Satin Slipper* (Sheed & Ward, London), translation.
       Blackfriars, 'Claudel & his Satin Slipper', October.
       Blackfriars, 'Psychology of Shakespeare', review of *Shakespeare's Way, A Psychological Study*, by Revd F. C. Kolbe, February.
       Blackfriars, 'Notes on St Joan & Bernard Shaw', July.
1932   *A Daily Hymn Book* (Burns Oates & Washbourne, London), contributor.
       Poems: Original & Derived (Lonsdale & Bartholomew, Bradford).
       Christ the King (Catholic Truth Society, London), March.
       Ave Maria, 'Notes & remarks on the original of Chesterton's Fr Brown', 14 May.
       Blackfriars, 'Wowsers', July.
1933   Claudel, Paul, *Ways & Crossways* (Sheed & Ward, London), translation.
       The Ampleforth Journal, 'Paul Claudel', vol. xxxvii.

Catholic Truth and *Catholic Book Notes*, 'The Latest from the Land of Youth', review of *Twenty Years a-Growing* by Maurice O'Sullivan, Sept.–Oct.

Two Hundred Folk Carols edited by Sir Richard R. Terry (Burns Oates & Washbourne, London), contributor.

1934   *G. K.'s Weekly*, 'Problem Plays of Claudel', 1 February.

G. K.'s Weekly, 'Confession, by Paul Claudel', 11 October, translation.

1935   *The Douai Magazine*, 'Some Pressed Flowers from Old Douai', vol. viii, autumn.

1936   *The Downside Review*, 'Gilbert Keith Chesterton, Only a Memory', vol. liv.

The Venerabile, 'La Magliana', vol. vii, no. 4, April.

The Douai Magazine, 'Joseph Robert Cowgill Bishop of Leeds, 1911–1936. A Memoir', vol. ix, no. 2.

1937   *Father Brown on Chesterton* (Frederick Muller, London).

The Downside Review, 'Gilbert Keith Chesterton', vol. lv, January.

Blackfriars, 'Claudel Dramatist', February.

Blackfriars, 'Claudel Dramatist', April.

The Tablet, 'The Scholarly Approach to English', 22 May.

The Downside Review, 'A Book about Shaw', review of *Shaw. George versus Bernard* by G. P. Hackett, vol. lv, October.

The Douai Magazine, 'Christmas 1883', vol. ix, autumn.

1938   Father Brown's Ghost Stories (unpublished).

The Downside Review, 'Veni Sancte Spiritus; Stabat Mater', translation, April.

1939   *Collects and Prefaces from the Missal* (Catholic Truth Society, London), May, translation.

The Douai Magazine, 'Saint Benedict', poem, vol. x, no. 4.

The Douai Magazine, 'Canon John James Hally (1885–89)', vol. x, no. 4.

The Downside Review, 'Trial of Jesus Christ', vol. lvii.

1940   *The Downside Review*, 'Some footnotes to the life of Père Lamy, Pt. 1', from Maurice Berthon's *Three Months with Père Lamy*, vol. lviii, April.

The Downside Review, 'Some footnotes to the life of Père Lamy, Pt. 2', July.

The Venerabile, 'The Rt. Rev. William Giles', vol. ix, no. 4, April.

A Month of Sundays: The Foolishness of Father Brown (T. Geoghegan, Bradford).

1941   *The Venerabile*, 'Monte Porzio Catone', vol. x, no. 2, November.

1943   *Blackfriars*, 'Review of Gill's *Last Essays*', vol. 24, February.

1944   *Blackfriars*, 'Playmate of the Universe', Review of *Gilbert Keith Chesterton*, by Maisie Ward, June.

The Douai Magazine, 'David Bede Ryan, O. S. B.', spring.

1946   *Jerome Savonarola* (Blackfriars, Oxford).

The 19th Century, 'G. K. Chesterton. Recognita Decennalia', June (by 'Father Brown').

1948   *The Douai Magazine*, 'Old Douai', spring.

1951   Biver, Comte Paul, *Père Lamy* (Clonmore & Reynolds, Dublin), revised and enlarged translation.

Appendix II

Alphabetical list of paintings and drawings in Father O'Connor's art collection sold at auction on 12 June 1913, British Galleries, Bradford; 28 July 1950, Christie & Co., London; 3 and 4 December 1952, Ernest de Rome, Bradford.

Apol, Louis, *Desolation*, drawing, 1950.
Alunno, Niccolò, *The Crucifixion*, on panel, arched top, 1950.
Baroccio, Federigo, *Our Saviour*, on panel, arched top, 1950.
Barrett, George, *Lake and Trees with setting Sun*, drawing, 1952.
Becker, Georges, *Impressionist Haymaking*, 1952.
Beverley, William Roxby, *Landscape with Storm Clouds*, drawing, 1952.
Bonheur, Rosa, *Horses in a Field*, on panel, 1952.
Bonington, Richard Parkes, *Hannibal Crossing the Alps* and *Lake with Boats and Figures, Cumberland*, 1952.
Boucher, François, *Charity*, 1950.
Brabazon, H., *Coastal Outline*, drawing, 1952.
Breakspeare, William A., *Nude Lady Startled by a Crab*, 1952.
Breenbergh, Bartholomeus, *Biblical figure with landscape*, 1952.
Brewer, Adrian, *Portrait of a Flemish Gentleman, long beard, large hat and a red cloak*, on panel, 1952.
Brouwer, Adriaen, *A Peasant Holding Bagpipes*, 1950.
Brueghel, *The Adoration of the Magi*, drawing, 1950.
Bright, Henry, *Lake and Mountain landscape*, drawing, 1952.

Carmichael, James Wilson, *The Pilot Boat*, 1913.

Carracci, *Landscape with Classical Ruins and the Angel appearing to St Jerome*,1950.

Cattermole, George, *Lake and Mountain, Castle and group of Figures*, drawing, 1952.

Charles, James, *The River Meadow*, 1913.

Constable, John, *Dedham Mill*, 1913.

A Study for *The Ponds, Hampstead Heath*, on paper, 1950.

A Landscape, with pool, on panel, 1950.

Cattle and Storm Clouds, 1952.

Ploughing and Rainbow, Sevenoaks, Kent, 1952.

Landscape with Cattle, drawing, 1952.

Cortona, Joseph, *Madonna and Child*, 1952.

Cotman, John Joseph, *An Autumn River Scene*, drawing, 1950.

Cowper, Samuel, *The Great Lord Fairfax*, 1913.

Cox, David, *River Conway from Llanfrind*, 1913.

Creswick, Thomas, *English Pastoral*, 1913.

Waterfall at Powerstown, Co. Wicklow, 1952.

Da Imola, Innocenzo, *The Madonna and Child, with Saints Francis and Bonaventure*, on panel, 1950.

Daubigny, Charles François, *Peasant Carrying Basket*, drawing, 1952.

Dawson, Henry Thomas, Snr, *Evening*, 1913.

De Heem, Cornelis, *A Lobster, Wine Glass and Fruit on a Table*, 1950.

De Largillière, Nicolas, *Portrait of Lord Clare, Marshal of France*, 1952.

Della Francesca, Piero, *Portrait of a Lady, in yellow embroidered dress and white head-dress*, on panel, 1950.

Dupre, (Leon) Victor, *Homeward Bound the Coming Storm*, 1952.

Ellis, Edwin, An early watercolour, 1913.

Village Scene, drawing, 1952.

Etty, William, *The Bather*, 1913.

Nude Woman Drying her Feet, on panel, 1952.

Fielding, Copley, *Wooded landscape, Storm Clouds*, drawing, 1952.

Finch, Francis Oliver, *Flight into Egypt*, drawing, 1952.

Fisher, Mark, *Sheep in Meadow with Trees*, 1952.

Flink, Govert, *The Money Changer*, portrait, 1952.

Florentine school, *The Crucifixion*, on panel, 1950.

Francia, Francesco, *The Madonna and Child, with Two Angels*, on panel, 1950.

Garofalo, *The Crowning of St Catherine by the Infant Saviour*, on panel, 1950.

G. N., *Landscape with Cottage*, on panel, 1952.

Goyder, Alice Kirkby, *Still Life, Autumn Berry Sprays*, drawing, 1952.

Graham, George, *Versailles*, 1952.

Gunett, *Landscape with figures and covered wagon*, 1952.

Hardin, *Fruit*, still life, on panel, 1952.

Harpignies, Henri Joseph, *Soliel Couchant le Sentier*, 1952.

Heeremans, Thomas, *Peasants outside a Tavern*, signed and dated 1685, 1950.

Henderson (?), *A Mail Cart on a Road*, 1950.

Hill, James John, *Evening Pastoral*, 1913.

Horlor, Joseph, *Landscape with Lake*, 1952.

Ibbetson, Julius Caesar, *A Landscape, with cottage and peasant on a road*, on panel, 1950.

Jonson, Cornelis (van Ceulen), *Portrait of Sarah Harrington, afterwards Lady Hastings, in a black embroidered dress and large white lawn ruff and black and white head-dress*, dated 1628, on panel, 1950.

Kite, Joseph Milner, *Naked Boy in a Vineyard*, 1952.

Knight, John William Buxton, 1913:

In the Hayfield
Showery Spring, academy picture 1875
By the Canal
Evening on the Heath
Rain Passing Over
Summer Smouldering, Chorley Wood Moor
Path Through the Fir Woods
Twilight in the Pines
1952:
Coast scene. Stream and Landscape
Landscape with Sheep in Meadow and Cottage

Haymaking by Twilight
Seascape with Barge and Sailing Ships
Gathering Flowers
Sunset with Storm Clouds
Moorland Landscape
Tree-lined Avenue
Storm Clouds
Huntsmen in Woodland Scene
Landscape, Chorley Wood, Herts.
Evening, Chorley Wood Common (lot included two unnamed pictures)
Moorland with Monument
1952 drawings:
Seascape with Jetty
Landscape
Saltaire
Chopping Turnips
Through the Meadows
The Hunt, To the Cover
Old Basing, Hants
River Colne, West Drayton
Early Morning, Poole
Village Scene

Lely, Sir Peter, *Portrait of a man in black with a white collar*, 1952.

Linnell, John, *Sheep Feeding at a Rack*, 1952.

Linthorst, Jacobus, *Flowers in a Terracotta Vase, with bird's nest on a marble slab*, signed and dated 1789, 1950.

Luini, Bernardino, *Portrait of a Young Lady*, on panel, 1952.

MacCullum, Andrew, *Palace of the Caesars, Rome*, drawing, 1952.

Macdonald, John Blake, Medieval figure subject, 1952.

Manlon, A., *Apple Blossom by Lakeside*, 1952.

Marcellis. O., *Fruit, Bird's Nest, Birds and Insects*, 1950.
Herbage with Snake and Butterflies, 1950.

Meason, W. F., *Barges on the Thames*, drawing, 1952.

Mettling, L., *Portrait of a Girl, in a dark dress*, 1950.

Mignard, Pierre, *Portrait of Molière, in black dress and plum-coloured cloak*, 1950.

Millais, Sir John Everett, *A Woody Lane Scene*, drawing, 1950.

Moore, Henry, *Winter Sunset – Yarmouth*, 1913.
  Land in Sight, 1913.

Morland, George, *Oxford seen from Headington*, on panel, 1952.

Morley, G. W., *Market Scene in Picardy*, 1952.

Muller, G. E., *Moorland landscape Storm with Clouds*, 1952.

Müller, William James, *Leigh Woods, Bristol*, 1913.
  A Grecian Landscape, 1950.
  1950 drawings:
  Ladies and Gentlemen
  Valley Scene with bridge over a river
  A View in Greece
  A Hilly River Scene with tower and figures

Nicholson, W (?illiam), *A Lake Scene*, drawing, 1950.

Niemann, Edmund John, *A View near Nottingham*, 1950.
  1950 drawings:
  A View near the Coast, with troops on a road
  A View near Nottingham
  Plymouth, Coast Scene, 1952.

Penley, (Edwin) A., *A Castle, with stream and bridge*, drawing, 1950.

Pintoricchio, *The Holy Family with the Infant St John, in a landscape*, on panel, 1950.

Pocock, Nicholas, *Naval Battle, 1794*, on panel, 1952.

Priestman, Bertram, *The Iris Pool*, 1913.
  River Scene and Tug, 1913.
  Fading Roses, still life, 1952.
  Ludlow Bridge and River, 1952.

Pyne, James Baker, *Seaside Sketch*, 1913.
  Rainmaking in Connaught, 1913.

Reynolds, Joshua, *Portrait of the Artist in Red Coat*, 1952.

Richardson, Thomas Miles, *Autumnal Sunrise*, 1913.

Rigaud, Hyacinthe, *Portrait of a Cavalier*, 1952.

Rutherford, *Janet*, portrait, 1952.

Sambaugh, A. D., *Ships in Harbour, Low Tide*, drawing, 1952.
Schofield, Kershaw, *Flowers*, still life, 1952.
Sickert, Bernard, French Impressionist Scene, 1952.
Smith, John Brandon, *Landscape of Rolling Hills and Figures*, drawing, 1952.
Stott, Edward, 1952 drawings:
  Child Picking Flowers
  Flight into Egypt
  The Downs, Amberley
Syer, John, *Moel Siabod*, 1913.
Teniers, David, Snr, *St Anthony in the Desert*, on copper panel, 1952.
Terburg, Gerhard, *Portrait of a Gentleman, in black dress with white lawn collar*, 1950.
Troyon, Constant, *Children with Goats*, 1950.
Turner, Joseph Mallord William, *Onset of the Squall*, 1913.
  Afterglow, sketch in oil, 1913.
  The Thames below London, sketch in oil, 1913.
  Set of three small landscape sketches.
Seascape with Storm Clouds, 1952.
  Two – Seascape and Landscape
Unknown 1952:
  Village and landscape, on panel.
  Flowers in Vase, pair, still life, 8? ins x 10? ins.
  Flowers in Vase, pair, still life, 9? ins x 12? ins
  Fruit and Flowers, still life.
  Landscape with Farm Cart and Sheep
  Portrait Henry VIII
  Man on a Donkey, landscape, on panel.
  Dutch Town with Church.
  Elijah, in red cloak, fed by ravens.
  Madonna and Child, with figures in panel at base and top corners.
  Landscape and Winding River, on panel.
  Portrait of a Nun in a White Habit.
  Carisbrook Castle, Isle of Wight.
  Holy Mary, on panel, Greek.

Christ Crowned with Thorns, on panel, Flemish.

1952 drawing.

Moorland Landscape with Farm Buildings.

Van Cleve, Joos, A triptych, with a *Descent from the Cross* in the centre, with the *Magdalen and a Saint* on the wings. On panel, centrepiece with arched top, 1950.

Van Dyck, Anthony, *Portrait of Frans Snyders, by chair*, on panel, 1950.

Van Huysum, Jan, *Flowers*, 1950.

Van Mierevelt, Michiel, *Portrait of a Lady, aged 34, in black dress with embroidered stomacher, white lawn ruff and lace coif and gold chain*, with inscription and date 1628, signed. On panel, 1950.

Varley, John, *Llanberis*, 1913.

1950 drawing:

River Scene with angler and two other figures.

Verboeckhoven, Eugene Joseph, *Donkey, Goat and Kid*, 1913.

Veronese School, *The Mocking of Christ*, on panel, 1950.

Villiers, Huet, *Self-portrait*, drawing, 1952.

Vincent, George, Landscape, 1913.

Watson, George Spencer, Nude study, 1952.

Willis, H. Brittan, *Farmstead and Landscape near Bognor*, drawing, 1952.

Wilson, Richard, *Italian Landscape*, 1913.

Scene on the Alban Lake, 1913.

Great Fall at Tivoli, 1913.

Portrait of the artist, in dark coat with red cap, holding palette and brushes, on panel, 1950.

Wissing, Willem, *Portrait of Lady Burghley (as a young girl)*, 1952.

Bibliography

Albert, S. M., 'John O'Connor', *Blackfriars*, vol. 33, January–December.

Belloc, Hilaire, Hilaire Belloc–Elizabeth Belloc Correspondence, Georgetown University Library, Washington DC.

Benedictines of Stanbrook Abbey, *In A Great Tradition* (John Murray, London, 1956).

Bible, Song of Solomon, *The Song of Songs* (Golden Cockerel Press, Waltham St Lawrence, 1925), Preface.

Biver, Comte Paul, *Père Lamy* (Clonmore & Reynolds, Dublin, 1951).

Bradford English Society, West Riding Archives 39D85.

Brown, Alfred, 'A Layman's Tribute', *Yorkshire Catholic Monthly*, March 1952.

Cartwright Memorial Hall, West Riding Archives 68D88.

Chesterton, G. K., *Autobiography* (Hutchinson, London, 1936).

Chesterton, G. K., 'A Book of War-Songs', *The Speaker*, 1 June 1901.

Chesterton, G. K., *The Complete Father Brown Stories* (Wordsworth Editions, Ware, Hertfordshire, 1989).

Chesterton, G. K., 'A Note on Father Brown', *The Heaton Review*, vol. vii, 1934.

Corrigan, Felicitas, *Letter to Father Ignatius*, Stanbrook Abbey Archives, Worcester.

Gatty, Charles, *George Wyndham Recognita* (John Murray, London, 1917).

Gill, Eric, *Autobiography* (Lund Humphries, London, 1992).

Gill, Eric, *Diaries, 1898-1949* (Tate Britain Library, Microfiche filmed by the Photographic Department of the University of California, Los Angeles).

G. K. Chesterton Papers, vol.xi, British Library MSS Add 73196.

G. K. Chesterton Papers, vol. ii, British Library MSS Add 73187.

Guinness, Alec, *Blessings in Disguise* (Hamilton, London, 1985).

Heenan, John Carmel, *Cardinal Hinsley* (Burns, Oates & Washbourne, London, 1944).

Jones, David, 'The Kensington Mass', *Agenda,* vol.12, Pt 1, 1973-4.

L' Artisan Liturgique. July–September 1938, National Art Library, MSL/1995/17/6/1.

Mackenzie, Compton, *Octave Seven 1931-38* (Chatto & Windus, London, 1968).

Mackey, Aidan, 'Diary of Frances Chesterton 1904-5', *The Chesterton Review,* vol. xxv, August 1999.

O'Connor, John, *Annals of the Poor,* PR4453.Z99 P3 M3, G. K. Chesterton Collection, John M. Kelly Library, University of St Michael's College, Toronto.

O'Connor, John, 'Christmas 1883', *The Douai Magazine,* vol. ix, Autumn 1937.

O'Connor, John, 'Claudel, Dramatist', *Blackfriars,* vol.18, February, April, 1937.

O'Connor, John, *Correspondence with Charles Gatty,* Downside Abbey Archives.

O'Connor, John, *Correspondence with Dame Werburg Welch, 1936-51,* WW/D2 Stanbrook Abbey Archives, Worcester.

O'Connor, John, 'Eric Gill: The searcher for Reality. A Personal Impression of the Artist', *The Bookman,* December 1930.

O'Connor, John, *Father Brown on Chesterton* (Frederick Muller, London, 1937).

O'Connor, John, *Father Brown's Ghost Stories,* PR4453.C4Z99 F3 M3 SMRC,

G. K. Chesterton Collection, John Kelly Library, University of St Michael's College, Toronto.

O'Connor, John, *Father Brown's Mixed Memories,* PR4453.C4Z99 F33 1920 SMRC, G. K. Chesterton Collection, John Kelly Library, University of St Michael's College. Toronto.

O'Connor, John, 'The Infancy of Father Brown', *The Sower,* July 1928.

O'Connor, John, *Letter to Eric Gill,* 9 November 1928, Tate Gallery Archives, TGA 8129.2

O'Connor, John, *A Month of Sundays: The Foolishness of Father Brown* (T. Geoghegan, Bradford, 1940).

O'Connor, John, 'Old Douai', *The Douai Magazine,* spring 1948.

O'Connor, John, *Papers of John O'Connor,* PR4453 C4 Z99 P3 M3, G.K. Chesterton Collection, John M. Kelly Library, University of St Michael's College, Toronto.

O'Connor, John, 'Paul Claudel', *Ampleforth Journal,* vol. xxxvii, 1933.

O'Connor, John, 'Problem Plays', *G. K.'s Weekly,* 1 February 1934.

O'Connor, John, 'Some Pressed Flowers from Old Douai', *The Douai Magazine,* vol. viii, autumn 1935.

O'Connor, John, 'Review of Last Essays of Eric Gill', *Blackfriars,* vol. 24, February 1943.

O'Connor, John, STP, *The Weld Sermon* (Downside Abbey, Bath, 1913).

O'Connor, John, *Why Revive the Liturgy and How?* (Published for private circulation only, probably around 1928).

Parker, Stanley, 'Monsignor John O'Connor or A Character Comes To Life', *Yorkshire Observer,* 25 February 1941.

Redmond, James, 'Monsignor John Prior', *The Venerabile,* vol.iii, October 1926.

Right Rev. Mgr. J. O'Connor, *The Douai Magazine,* vol. xvii, spring 1952.

Rothenstein, John, *Summer's Lease, Autobiography 1901–1938* (Hamish Hamilton, London, 1965).

Scott, Christina, *A Historian and his World: A Life of*

Christopher Dawson 1889-1970 (Sheed & Ward, 1984).

Shewring, Walter, (ed.), *Letters of Eric Gill* (Cape, London, 1947).

Speaight, Robert, *The Life of Eric Gill* (Methuen, London, 1966).

Spender, J. A., *Sir Robert Hudson; A Memoir* (Cassell & Co., London, 1930).

Thompson, Francis, *The Mistress of Vision* (Douglas Pepler, Ditchling, 1918).

Ward, Maisie, *Gilbert Keith Chesterton*, (Sheed & Ward, London, 1944).

Wyndham, Guy, (comp.) *Letters of George Wyndham, 1877-1913* (T & A Constable, Edinburgh, 1915).

Index

Lightning Source UK Ltd.
Milton Keynes UK
23 April 2010

153197UK00001BA/2/P